A WOLF'S MOON

A Helicopter Pilot's Story

HANK SANDS

Agio
PUBLISHING HOUSE

Agio
PUBLISHING HOUSE

151 Howe Street, Victoria BC Canada V8V 4K5

For rights information and bulk orders, please contact
info@agiopublishing.com
or go to
www.agiopublishing.com

Visit Hank Sands' website at *www.awolfsmoon.com.*

A Wolf's Moon
ISBN 978-1-897435-72-4 (trade paperback)
ISBN 978-1-897435-73-1 (ebook)

Cataloguing information available from
Library and Archives Canada.
Printed on acid-free paper.
Agio Publishing House is a socially responsible company,
measuring success on a triple-bottom-line basis.
10 9 8 7 6 5 4 3 2 1

DEDICATION

To my wife, Linda, naturally! You are always there for me.

Also, thanks to a long list of family and friends who helped me along the way.

TABLE OF CONTENTS

Introduction   1

Chapter One   In the Beginning   3

Chapter Two   Hard Lessons   17

Chapter Three   Henry the Buffalo   37

Chapter Four   Those Amazing Whooping Cranes   49

Chapter Five   Message in a Bottle   57

Chapter Six   The Moil for Gold   73

Chapter Seven   The Mad Irishman   91

Chapter Eight   Dead Reckoning   107

Chapter Nine   The Bell Jet Ranger   121

Chapter Ten   A Wolf's Moon   131

Chapter Eleven   Cross Roads   145

Chapter Twelve   All's Well That Ends Wells   155

Chapter Thirteen   Avalanche Control   171

Chapter Fourteen   The Ghost of Old Growler   187

Chapter Fifteen   Battle Fatigue   199

Chapter Sixteen   Down, But Not Out   209

Chapter Seventeen   A New Beginning   215

Author's Notes and
Acknowledgements   225

INTRODUCTION

During my eighteen-year career flying helicopters, I spent almost a year airborne holding onto the controls of many different types of "choppers." Northern Canada was my home for most of that time, where I flew with the most adventurous of human beings often surrounded by an un-caged zoo of amazing animals.

I fell flat on my face a few times, but always managed to get up and carry on with this incredible flying experience. These stories are a composite of tales based on the truth. I've taken a fair amount of leeway with the human characters, even embellished them a bit, but the bears, wolves, moose, buffalo and other creatures performed pretty much as I've written.

Hopefully, there are still lots of people alive out there who are in these tales. Some of them might say, "I didn't behave that way." Or, "It didn't happen quite the way you've written it." But one thing is for certain – they will all say, "That sure did happen!"

CHAPTER ONE

IN THE BEGINNING

The airspeed indicator read 260 knots and I was 1000 feet above the end of runway 06. The old CF-100 jet interceptor groaned as I put it into an eighty degree hard turn to port and popped the dive brakes. In seconds, I was 180 degrees downwind with the airspeed rapidly falling below 200 knots. I closed the dive brakes – huge claw-like flaps that opened on the top and bottom of the wings and which almost turned the aircraft into a rock. If they failed to close, my navigator and I would have just seconds to eject. Simultaneously, I dropped the landing gear and flaps while continuing my steep turn and descending rapidly. At 200 feet, I quickly levelled the aircraft, reducing airspeed and landed smoothly on the runway.

At last I was once again holding onto the controls of a jet fighter after a three-year ground tour as a radar controller at Beaver Bank, Nova Scotia, a small base 25 miles north of Halifax. I taxied towards the hanger and the long line of parked Electronic Warfare Unit [EWU] CF-100s at

Royal Canadian Air Force Station St. Hubert close to Montréal. In its heyday, as an operational air force station, it was host to 416 and 425 All Weather Fighter Squadrons flying CF-100s. From 1958 to 1961, I had the privilege of flying the grand old bird out of 409 Squadron at Comox, BC. St. Hubert was also the permanent home to Air Defence Command Headquarters which controlled all the RCAF fighter and interceptor squadrons in Canada and Europe.

As my navigator, Dan Buckler, and I walked into the flight operations room with our helmets under our arms, we noticed a large group of our fellow pilots and navigators crowded around the operations bulletin board looking at a typed memorandum. Curious, we elbowed our way through the grimly silent group. The memo was dated Tuesday, April 14, 1964 and read as follows:

> **Attention: All Aircrew**
>
> *It has been determined by the Federal Government that we have an excess of aircrew in our command. Therefore it is our intention to release 500 aircrew from the RCAF within three months. 250 will be in an 18-month seniority bump created by a build-up of aircrew during the Cuban crisis, and 250 within two years of retirement. Those scheduled for release will be notified in one week.*

A chill went through my body as I remembered the rumours of cutbacks. A few days before this, Dan and I were returning from a late night of Montreal pub crawling when we noticed that every light on every floor of the huge Air Defence Command Headquarters building was on.

"Something bad is happening up there," Dan had said, giving me one of his intuitive looks.

The CF-100 and Flight Lieutenant Hank Sands.

We'd both survived a three-year tour on different radar sites and were on temporary duty here, waiting to be recycled back to the new CF-101 Voodoos, the American airplane that had replaced the CF-100 as Canada's operational interceptor. Both our wives and children were in Ottawa waiting for us to take our training and settle down on one of Canada's many airbases. For months, I had been staying at St. Hubert all week and driving to Ottawa on weekends.

One week later, all of us watched as the names were posted. I couldn't believe my eyes. Both Dan and I were on the list along with almost a third of the EWU crew. In three months, we would be thrown out with a mere three months' extra pay and allowances. Those who weren't on the list were all thinking, "When will my turn come?"

One day I was planning a long career in the Air Force and the next I was trying to decide what to do with the rest of my life. Dan, who ended up in Calgary and became a lifelong friend, pretty much said what we all were feeling at the time, "To go from an RCAF Flight Lieutenant to peon status is hard on my fragile self-esteem and ego." We had both been Flight Lieutenants.

I finally decided to return to the city where I was born – Vancouver, British Columbia. My wife Melba, my two kids and I ended up living in a run-down RV Park in Mallardville, a small community outside of the big city.

Due to the severe housing shortage in Ottawa, I had purchased a 10 by 50 foot motor home for my family to live in there. It had been towed from Ottawa at Air Force expense, but they refused to pay for the three blown tires. I felt like one of those tires. Linda, Melba's daughter who I had adopted, was eleven years old and my son Jeff was five.

After two months of living off the meagre severance pay and allowances I finally got down to the serious business of looking for work. I was angry and disillusioned. I had absolutely no interest in flying anymore. I looked at many different career options. I applied and was accepted into UBC on a Batchelor of Science program. I also filled out many Federal Government application forms, which included Customs Agent and Indian Agent. I even entered a Provincial competition to become a Conservation officer and managed to get on the short list.

"I'll get you a job as a deck hand and you can work your way up to captain of a tugboat in no time," my mother said. She was office manager of a company that did all the hiring for the towboat industry. No doubt I would have landed one of these quiet uneventful careers if it weren't for a small advertisement in the classified section saying:

Helicopter pilot training

Northwest Helicopters

Pitt Meadows, B.C.

Lenny Peters, president of the company, answered the phone with a brisk, "Ya!"

There was giggling in the background, which must have been his secretary and staff.

"I want to look into helicopter training," I said.

"I'm pretty busy right now," he replied gruffly. "Meet me in my office tomorrow at ten sharp."

"Uh, where's that?" I asked.

"Mary's Café at Pitt Meadows Airport," he said and hung up.

I drove out there first thing in the morning. His office was a well-worn stool in the little restaurant at the small Pitt Meadows airport. The waitress was skinny and mean and the coffee was awful.

Lenny arrived at 10:30 dressed like he'd just come off a very proper golf course, but he soon lit up the greasy space with words of awe about the helicopter industry.

"Flying airplanes is hours of boredom with moments of sheer terror. Flying helicopters is hours of sheer terror," Lenny said. "If you want to fly them, you'd better marry them."

I was to learn that Lenny was full of these kinds of trite expressions. He even managed the old saying, "There are old pilots and bold pilots, but no old, bold pilots."

He owned the helicopter sitting outside this grungy airport café that served as his office. If I was going to learn to fly helicopters this company was the best bargain around.

"After you graduate from my class there'll be lotsa jobs waiting for you," he said with all the confidence of a car salesman. "Now let's go take a ride."

He led me across a field littered with old Cessnas, Pipers and a weathered Second World War B-25. All were tied to the ground with frayed wire attached to cement blocks. Any decent wind would have sent them all flying on their own. The helicopter glistened like a Nile jewel amongst this collection of relics.

"She's like brand new," Lenny said proudly. "Used to be a Bell 47 G1, but my last student dumped it off a raft into 20 feet of water. Helicopters have ten times the moving parts of a similar-sized fixed wing aircraft and we had to replace most of them. Got her all fixed up. Now it's called a Bell 47 G1A. It has new hydraulic controls that make it much smoother to fly."

The helicopter sat on two sturdy metal tubes fore and aft of the engine. Welded to these tubes were skids that looked to be made of the same material. A roughly 2-foot by 6-foot steel frame made of welded tubing was strapped to the cross tubes with clamps. Tie down hooks were welded to the tubes much like hooks on a truck box. The inside of the frame was filled with heavy nylon netting.

"These cargo racks were probably invented during the Korean War to carry injured men," Lenny said. "If you've ever watched the *M.A.S.H.* TV series this machine is very close to the model they used. Every thing has to be loaded evenly on both sides. I have no doubt that they never had a problem finding two injured men at one time. When two big men and the pilot sit in that cabin there's absolutely no room for anything else. Everything has to be tied to these cargo racks with lengths of braided cotton rope because it's strong and holds a knot. Each is cut to a length that is just short of tangling with the tail rotor should it come undone. Also designed to help keep the tail rotor out of trouble are those bear paws on the back of the skids." He pointed at two flat metal pads shaped like elongated delta wings. "They're named after snowshoes and serve the same purpose in snow or soft ground. The tail rotor is the most fragile moving part on this helicopter. Let me show you."

I followed him back to the tail rotor where he pointed at a small metal tab on the tip of each blade. "A high patch of grass is enough to bend these tabs. If they're broken off the tail rotor is scrap metal along with a lot of other moving parts."

I was beginning to wonder about flying helicopters.

"What's that for?" I asked as we returned to the side of the helicopter. The look he gave me made me feel like I'd just come out of kindergarten. Tied to the nylon net was a hand pump. It had a long rubber hose with a hooked nozzle on the outlet and a long pipe stem sticking out of the intake.

"Bet you Air Force guys never put fuel in an aircraft," he replied a little sarcastically.

He was right. I'd watched lots of Air Force aircraft being refuelled, but always from a comfortable distance. Then he opened a small aluminium door on a compartment built into the tail rotor boom just behind the engine. He took out a large galvanized funnel lined with something that looked like leather and an odd looking wrench.

"That pump is used to refuel the helicopter. This funnel is lined with chamois to help keep out water and dirt," he said in his all-knowing voice. "If you want to become a helicopter pilot you'd better be prepared to be refuelling out of 45-gallon drums 90% of the time. There's millions of them scattered all over the North. Most of the flying you're going to be doing will be in the middle of nowhere where there's no airports.

"And those drums which weigh close to 400 pounds are usually lying on their sides to keep the water out so you better have a strong back. This bung wrench is used to open those drums, if you're lucky. You're also going to see lots of 10-gallon drums. In fact, you're going to be flying around a lot with one or two tied on each side of the racks to give you extra flying time. It's easier and faster than slinging a 45-gallon drum under you. Last year, I ended up on a job that had 200 ten-gallon drums. Couldn't budge the lids so had to cut holes in each drum with an axe. I prayed every time I hit that axe with a hammer. One spark and I would've been heaven bent."

He then pointed to the two round saddle tanks high above the engine. "Speaking of fuel, these two tanks hold 43 gallons of fuel altogether and the helicopter burns about 15 gals per hour. There's a cross feed so they both feed into the engine evenly. You can figure on flying about two and one half hours depending how much power you're pulling.

"The fuel gauges aren't too accurate so you'll be using a dipstick to check your fuel level. You'll also be opening these drain cocks on the bottom of the tanks to check for water before every flight," he added turning a valve that sent gas pouring on the ground.

"Airplanes usually cough and sputter a bit when they get a little water in the engine. Helicopter engines simply quit. Now let's take a look at the cockpit."

"Great," I said, not knowing if it was.

I was to learn later that this helicopter was indeed a very close relative to the one on the *M.A.S.H.* TV series. Bell Helicopters built about 18 different versions of this helicopter. In the following years I flew most of them, but this was the one I remembered best.

The cockpit was equipped with dual flying controls. Lenny slid in on the left side and me on the right. It was like sitting inside a big balloon. The view through the plastic bubble enclosing the cabin was only partially blocked by a small consol with about one tenth of the instruments I was used to looking at in a jet fighter.

"The two pedals by your feet control the pitch on the tail rotor," he said. "This control column between your legs is called the cyclic. It tilts the rotor in whatever direction you move it like a plate on a slippery table. The way you keep it from sliding off the table is by pulling in power and increasing the pitch on the rotors. The long lever on your left is called a collective. It has a motorcycle-like twist throttle to control power and RPM.

"Raising and lowering the lever controls the pitch to the rotor blades. The controls on the left are permanent and the ones on the right removable, giving you room to carry two passengers."

I took one look at the narrow cabin and wondered how two grown men could squeeze in.

"Pretty simple, aye?" he added. I thought it was anything but simple. He started the engine and the rotors slowly wound up. As he applied power and lifted off the ground I had a wonderful feeling of defying gravity. In just a few seconds, we were in forward flight flying over a quilt pattern of pastures and fields with row upon rows of vegetables and fruit trees.

There were also vast treeless fields where what looked like smoke drifted out of black holes. "Those are peat bogs," he shouted over the noisy engine. "There's fires burning deep down in that muskeg that will never go out."

I couldn't believe my eyes when we suddenly came upon a group of naked men and women playing volleyball in a large clearing surrounded by high trees.

"That's 'Sunny Trails,' local nudist colony," he said with a grin as he circled slowly over them. They were so intent on the game they never even looked up.

I was hooked. The flying bug had caught me again. I was sure that my training would include other flights over this spot more than once.

On October 2, 1964, I climbed back into Lenny's helicopter to begin training. Lenny flew us out to the middle of a large cow pasture. The machine seemed to fly by itself with almost no movement of his hands and feet. There was no intercom radio. All communications involved shouting over the engine noise.

"This is going to be a cinch," I said to myself. I had trained on a Harvard, one of the nastiest planes to fly that was ever built. My Air Force instructor used to say, "If you can fly this, you can fly anything."

"Are you ready?" Lenny shouted over the roar of the helicopter.

I put my feet on the pedals, grabbed the collective and gently manipulated the cyclic.

"You have control," he said.

I had anything but control! I felt like I was standing on the edge of a skyscraper with one foot on a huge rubber ball, one hand rubbing my belly and the other patting my head. It's lucky there weren't any cows in that pasture or they would have been running for their lives. I felt like a knight in shining armour that'd lost his lance. How had it looked so easy?

This thing defied all logic and left my haughtiness in one of the cow pies that I bounced off several times. One hour per day was all I could manage at first. I would drive home rung out and dripping in sweat.

Slowly and painfully, my skill improved. I learned to hover in the same field and later between the first two cow pies that Lenny picked out, and finally more or less on one spot.

"Hovering is the first and the hardest thing to learn," Lenny told me and I believed him until I attempted my first approach and landing.

In forward flight the helicopter behaved like an airplane, but getting from there to a hover was not a simple matter of closing the throttle, settling on the runway and stepping on the brakes. It was more like landing with the wheels up on a hard runway. Huge amounts of power and control movements were required to bring this errant flying machine to a stop in a hover. Then you had to get the shaky brute on the ground.

"Let me show you an auto-rotation," he shouted out of the blue one day, pushing the collective down and closing the throttle. The engine was still running, but the rotors were free-wheeling. It was much like shifting to neutral in an automobile and coasting. I was used to gliding in airplanes with engines at idle, but nothing prepared me for this. We were falling like a rock.

At the last second, just before I thought we were going to crash, he rotated the machine violently on its tail and levelled off. We hit the ground skidding and thumping over the wet grass and cow pies.

"Now you know how it's done we won't be doing any more of them," he said when we finally came to a stop in one piece. I sensed he was as shaken up as I.

It was only years later when I became an instructor myself that I would learn that in the helicopter world, auto-rotations separated the men from the boys.

It took me about two hours longer than most of the trainees fresh off the street to go solo. No doubt it was because I had to unlearn a whole bunch of Air Force jet pilot habits, but from then on it was all downhill.

Unlike my Air Force instructors, Lenny rarely followed any sort of lesson plan. In fact he did everything on impulse. One day I was busy doing solo practice circuits over the airport when I saw him waving frantically next to the helipad, indicating he definitely wanted me to land.

I'd barely gotten settled on the helipad when he jumped into the helicopter and shouted, "We've got an emergency rescue mission. Take off and head for Sunny Trails."

"My God," I thought to myself, "one of those overweight volleyball players has had a heart attack."

The emergency turned out to be a couple of cute female skydivers who'd ended up drifting into a swamp less than a mile from the nudist colony. When we arrived they were standing up to their well developed bosoms in muddy water. We landed on the only solid ground for a mile around and they waded towards us dragging their chutes behind.

"Guess you'll fly them back to the airport and come back and get me," I said.

"Heck no," he replied. "They can sit on the skids."

I hate to think what would have happened to Lenny's licence if one of them had fallen off. It would have been the girl on my side because I was doing the flying and Lenny was firmly holding the hand of the other one. There were lots of people pointing and laughing when we arrived back at Pitt Meadows.

"Wash the mud off the skids," were Lenny's last words as he wandered off with the two girls, hand-in-hand.

And that's the way things went. Somehow, I managed to get the 25 hours required to add helicopters to my existing civilian commercial licence. Fortunately, I'd obtained that licence by taking a weekend course. Now I was $1625.00 poorer, but I was a licensed, qualified helicopter pilot.

"Now you can start earning some of that money back," Lenny told me. "I haven't been feeling too great lately and I have a few flying jobs that you can do for me. I'll start you off on easy stuff."

I was elated! I could build up some hours while I looked for a more permanent position. Hopefully, I wouldn't wreck his helicopter like his previous student had done.

During our training flights, Lenny had complained daily of stomach pains and I thought that I was the cause of it. Within a week poor Lenny was in the hospital. He died suddenly from cancer a month later. This left me with no job and no reference, but I knew that wouldn't be a problem. Hadn't Lenny said that helicopter companies were crying for pilots? It was time for me to start looking.

CHAPTER TWO

HARD LESSONS

I started job hunting with the biggest and the best, Okanagan Helicopters. Their office was based at Vancouver Airport. After a quick interview the personnel officer glared at me and said, "Why did you train with that guy and then come looking for a job with us?"

'That guy' was Lenny, obviously not held in high esteem by Canada's largest helicopter company. I think I blurted out something like, "Well, I didn't know any better."

I left that interview discouraged, figuring that I would have to continue looking around for other flying jobs. There were numerous small helicopter companies scattered all over the Vancouver area and I hit them all. I soon found out that there were lots of jobs out there, but no one was interested in hiring an ex-military jet jockey with a mere twenty-five helicopter flying hours under his belt.

"Go get some more flying experience and come back," the owner of Northern Helicopters told me. He owned a dozen helicopters compared to

Okanagan's 65 or more. How was I to do that? Weeks passed and no jobs turned up. I was ready to take my mother's advice and work my way up to captain of a tugboat when I received a phone call from the chief pilot of Okanagan Helicopters.

"We've decided we might take you on," he said.

After we sorted out the details, I left the phone and danced joyfully in circles with my kids.

I began advanced mountain training on Feb 16, 1965 in Kamloops (in BC's Interior) with several other pilots. We flew Bell 47 G2s almost identical to Lenny's machine. Not long after course completion I returned to Vancouver to get the great news that I was transferred to Okanagan's base at Nelson in BC's Kootenay region.

A week later, with my family stuffed in our Morris Mini Minor, I headed for Nelson. We followed a short distance behind our mobile home which was being towed by a nice older man with rusty truck. A big sign on our roof read, 'WIDE LOAD.' After a very long day, we finally arrived in Nelson.

The mobile home had blown two more tires and left a big piece of its rear bumper in a dip of the road at the Castlegar ferry crossing. We set it up in a small RV park with a nice view of the Kootenay River, which flowed out of the vast lake that it was named after. It was just five minutes drive to the base. I was ready to start my new career.

"This is a Hiller 12E," Don MacKenzie, the base manager, told me as he showed me the helicopter which sat on four little removable wheels in the rough built hanger. "It's a good workhorse, but you're not going to find it as smooth and easy to fly as those Bell 47s. This country is all rugged mountains and high tree lines with lots of bad weather to boot."

Don, with years of flying experience, had the responsibilities of running the base, flying his own helicopter missions and teaching me how to fly.

I made my first flight out of Nelson on the 14th of May. Don was right on all counts. The machine was a good workhorse, but it was like going from a Cadillac to a tractor. It took a couple of hours to learn to fly the beast. For the first week I did almost nothing except fly around with him and watch. Gradually, I was able to take on more responsibility. A second Hiller was sent up from Vancouver. I finally had my own machine and I thought I was up to every task assigned me.

Our biggest customer was the BC Forest Service. The Kootenay Lake area east of Nelson was prone to thunder storms and lightning strikes. That meant forest fires to fight.

Early in my training, Don lead me into the corner of the hanger where a rusty 45-gallon drum sat with its top cut out.

"This is a Monsoon Bucket," he said. "It was invented in the mid 1950s by Henry Stevenson, who owns a machine shop just a few blocks from here. We worked together for several years to get it operational."

Three steel cables were attached evenly to the rim, joined together to a single 20-foot cable that ended with a steel ring. The trap door on the bottom had an electric solenoid that was attached to a heavy rubber extension cord that ran the full length of the cable and could be plugged into a socket next to the cargo hook.

I was already familiar with the fact that all Okanagan helicopters had electrically operated hooks attached close to the centre of gravity beneath the machine to pick up and automatically release sling loads. A second button was installed on the cyclic to open the trap door in the bucket.

"If you notice there's a float on the edge of the trap door," he continued, turning the barrel on its side to show me. "The trick is to hit the water hard enough to close that door. Then, you hover backwards tipping the bucket on its side. Once it's full of water, away you go. One word of warning though. When you're ready to release the water over a burning snag, make sure you don't accidentally pull the cargo release button by mistake and lose the whole works."

It took me half a day's flying to master this contraption. Don was right! The trap door was hard to get closed and locked and it was easy to get the two switches mixed up. Forty-five gallons of water was a drop in the bucket on a roaring forest fire, but it was very effective on lightning strikes, provided water was close by. Fortunately, there were lots of lakes and ponds in the Kootenays. When we weren't hauling men and equipment out to fires or using our Monsoon bucket, we were taking forestry crews out to the mountain tops to cruise and evaluate timber resources.

The steep slopes and avalanche paths that supported only slide alder and huckleberry were usually the only openings big enough for us to land men. The lower, more protected slopes were so heavily forested there was almost nowhere to land.

Often we would have to hover with our skids sitting on a big rock with the rotors just inches from the slide and have the men jump out. Don was more up to this task than I was.

Early on in July, we got the exciting news that the National Ski Team was going to take summer training on the ever-frozen north slope of the Kokanee Glacier and they would use us exclusively for transportation. The glacier, which kept its snow cover year-round, was just 30 miles east of Nelson and was at the highest and most forbidding part of Kokanee Glacier Provincial Park.

Established in 1922, this was one of the oldest parks in the province. Around the turn of the century, discovery of small veins rich in gold and silver ore caused a local mining boom. Many of the park's trails were originally built by miners hauling ore and supplies. An old mile-high log cabin, which was nestled in the trees below the ski slope, served as a temporary cookhouse for the team who lived in tents while permanent buildings were being built. The miners who had built the cabin had followed an age-old commonsense tradition. They cut the trees down and used the logs to build the cabin in the area where they fell. It was only a matter of cutting out the scrub brush that had grown up over the years and we had a helipad right next to the cabin, maybe a little too close. I was to do my first big slinging job on July 25th. Using both helicopters Don and I hauled tons of lumber, ski equipment and bushels of food from a clearing close to an old walking trail that wound its way from the highway, at the edge of Kootenay Lake, directly to the cabin. It would have taken the pioneers all day to make this trip with packhorses. The round trip by helicopter took 20 minutes.

We used ten-foot-square, orange, braided-nylon nets with quick release hooks on three corners and a 5-inch steel ring on the fourth. The three snap hooks were attached to the ring once the net was loaded. A second 5-foot lanyard also with a snap hook and ring at each end of it would be snapped to the net. The ring was now ready to be hooked to the helicopter. A dozen nets were used with a crew at each end ready to load and unload them.

Helicopters are expensive to rent, so time was of the essence. The only time we landed was to refuel, which was about every 45 minutes. Aviation gasoline gas weighs 7.2 pounds per gallon so we kept the tanks less than half full to improve performance. A trained crewman hooked the ring to the helicopter while we hovered above him. He was always prepared to get a static shock because the air was cold and dry. Don told me he had heard of men getting knocked out from static shock from large helicopters in cold, dry blowing snow.

At the cabin, we simply released the load and headed back for more. It took eight hours to deliver everything they needed. It was piled in heaps beside the cabin. The team skied for a month. We kept them supplied with food and transported skiers with sprained ankles and such back to Nelson.

The ski team moved out on the first week of September. Even at this early date, signs of winter were everywhere and there had already been a dusting of new snow at the mile-high site. We spent a long day flying the team and all their equipment back to Nelson.

"Someone left their skis behind," Don told me on the 9th of September. "Pick them up on your way to Lardeau."

The cabin was pretty much enroute to the BC Forest Station at the head of Kootenay Lake, where I was transporting one young assistant forest ranger. I landed on the pad next to the now-deserted cabin for the hundredth time.

We quickly found the skis and a few other items, tied them on the cargo rack and took off. A cold wind descended down the slope. It took full power to climb ever so slowly away from the helipad. Suddenly, a downdraft hit me and down I went, spinning and sinking out of control.

In seconds, I was back on the pad in one piece beginning to breathe a sigh of relief when I heard the *rat-a-tat-tat* of the main rotors chewing a chunk out of the cabin. My young passenger didn't say a word, but he sure looked shaken.

"Sorry," was all I could think to say. We had no radio communication.

I spent a long day in a state of despair and shock, staring at the damaged helicopter rotors. During my years in the Air Force, I'd never so much as dented an airplane, but now after only seven months I'd severely damaged a helicopter.

Finally, towards evening I heard the familiar *chop-chop* of a helicopter arriving. Don circled over us several times then headed away waving at us to follow. We scrambled through thick brush and trees, guided only by the sound of the helicopter. The trees finally gave way to a treeless plateau where Don sat in the helicopter with the engine still running, close to the edge of a steep slope. The two of us ran the distance and scrambled aboard the helicopter. What a relief to not have to spend a night in that cabin!

"Did you tie the rotor down and disconnect the battery?" Don asked as I climbed in beside him. "Yes," I replied, relieved that he didn't hit me with a barrage of hysterical questions.

He applied full power. With the collective full up, and power at the red line, the Hiller still wouldn't leave the ground.

"Bad air," Don shouted over the noisy engine. "Dead air. I think I'm gonna have to take you out one at a time."

I hopped out and he took off with the young ranger. Even with the lighter load, the helicopter had to skim down the steep slope to get airborne.

The wind had died; it was cold and dead calm and at last I understood what Don had meant by "dead air." Long shadows were creeping across the long icy slope above me. It would be dark soon. I could still see a few flags and the deep ski-carved snow the ski team had left behind.

I was thinking that maybe I would be spending a night in the cabin alone when Don finally returned to pick me up. By the time I had my seat belt done up, Don had the helicopter up to full power. The helicopter didn't budge. The dead air that he had mentioned was now even deader. I was beginning to think we would both end up spending the night here.

"Hang on," he shouted, "you're about to learn something new and it's going to be hairy."

He eased down on the collective which allowed both the engine RPM and rotor speed to increase to the maximum and a little beyond. Then, without warning, he jerked the collective up. The helicopter jumped into the air and dove off the cliff. In seconds, the rotor speed was down to minimum and we were screaming down the steep slope like a runaway skier, dodging the taller shrubs. *My god,* I thought to myself! I'd survived one crash today and am now going to die in another. I wanted to scream, but I kept it inside. Don didn't need any distractions.

Finally, we had enough speed to get airborne and I was able to take my eyes off death's door and look at Don. He was completely unruffled because he knew what he was doing. I certainly didn't.

I learned my fate a week later. It was determined that the accident was a result of my inexperience and the unexpected downdraft. I was forgiven. The company decided that we needed a helicopter better suited to the high mountain terrain and sent us a newly re-built turbo charged Bell 47B. It had the same narrow cabin as the helicopter I'd trained on in Pitt Meadows, but unlike the Hiller it was designed for better high altitude performance. They said that it could maintain full power over halfway to the summit of Mount Everest if I should ever want to go there.

"There's a staking rush up in the Bugaboos, lots of helicopters involved," Don told me when I arrived one morning early in December. "Think you can handle flying a couple of prospectors around in ten feet of powder snow?"

"Sure thing," I said, glad to be off on something new.

Next morning, I took off with snowshoes strapped on the rack and lots of warm clothes.

The Bugaboo Mountain range between Nelson and Golden, BC, was famous for its long slopes of deep powder snow that attract the rich and famous every winter for helicopter skiing. It was also rich in minerals.

When I arrived in Golden there were already helicopters there from other companies. I was the only Okanagan pilot. We would fly prospectors out to stake claims each day. At night pilots and prospectors would get together, drink beer and gossip. We talked about everything except where we were staking each day. We were all friendly competitors wanting a bigger chunk of the land that surrounded a recently announced mineral strike. It was like the gold rush of old, except helicopters took the place of mules, horses, and rugged prospectors on foot.

The 11th of December dawned clear and cold. Tom Smith and Rick Follows, both experienced prospectors, were my passengers for the day. We took off early and headed straight for the area they wanted to stake. Never had I seen snow like this. Everywhere it was soft and fluffy as sifted flour and at least 10 feet deep. I tried landing in a big open meadow without success. As soon as the rotor blast hit the snow we were surrounded by a raging tornado of blinding whiteness. Once the skis were into the snow, the helicopter sank and sank until I was afraid that the tail rotor was going to dig into the snow and bend or break those fragile breakaway tabs that Lenny had first shown me. I finally found a spot on the edge of a creek where the wind had crusted the snow up a bit.

Even then the snow was halfway up the bubble before I felt settled in, but the tail rotor was hanging safely over the creek. The men struggled in the deep snow, but finally got their snowshoes on, picked up the white 4 by 4 stakes that were tied on the rack and trundled off to stake their claims.

When they finally returned the sun was getting low and the shadows were long and blue in the snow. Packs and snowshoes were quickly tied back on the racks and we all climbed happily into the warm helicopter. In a half hour or so we'd be back in Golden. By using full power I just managed to get the skids untangled from the snow and took off down the creek.

Immediately, there was a loud bang and the helicopter smashed into the creek bed on its side as if pounded by a giant fist. I was on top with Rick beneath me and poor Tom was squished by the two of us. In seconds, the three of us scrambled out into the snow through the shattered bubble. We all seemed unhurt. The first thing I noticed was a cleanly cut off dead snag that angled out over the creek. It had been well hidden in shadows, but it was obvious I'd hit it. As I looked at it in dismay, I lost the sight in my left eye.

"My god, I've lost an eye!" I remember screaming in shock and panic.

Tom came close and plucked a piece of plexiglas out of my forehead just above my eye. My blood had blinded me. A handful of snow quickly stopped the flow and I could see again. We stood staring dumbly at a fire burning in the red-hot turbo charger. Gasoline from a damaged fuel tank was dripping on it.

"Where's the bloody fire extinguisher?" I said to myself, climbing into the shattered cabin and looking about frantically. I finally found it strapped to the side of the instrument panel. With now frozen fingers I pulled frantically on the catch that held the extinguisher. It came off with a snap and I knew I'd have a good sized bruise where it hit my wrist. When I stepped back out through the bubble, Tom and Rick were nowhere to be found.

Wiser than me, they'd moved off a good distance to watch safely. They had decided that I'd earned the right to die if the helicopter blew up. The fire was almost touching the damaged fuel tank by now. The next hassle was getting the pin out of the trigger. I did it, finally. With a bruised hand and an almost dislocated finger I pointed and pulled. The fire was extinguished almost immediately.

I vowed to take a course on fire extinguishers in the near future. I now realized that we all should have run like hell as soon as we saw the fire, but ironically my foolishness not only saved the helicopter, it allowed us to retrieve our packsacks and snowshoes. We struggled through the neck-deep snow to a sawmill three miles away. The mill was sealed up for the winter, but we managed to scrounge up some food and get a fire going. First thing next morning, one of my fellow helicopter pilots picked us up.

He told me that when we hadn't turned up last night the whole group of prospectors and pilots had gathered in the pub, not so much to drink beer, but to figure out where we were. And they were very successful, thanks, no doubt, to the previous night's gossip.

The next day, Roy Webster flew in with an Okanagan Bell 204B from

Vancouver. This was a civilian version of the famous Vietnam Hueys so much in the news these days. Roy, a fellow ex-Air Force pilot, had been one of my instructors on the mountain course. It was a sad reunion. We flew into the accident site and I had the honour of hooking what was left my helicopter to the end of a long lanyard attached to the big helicopter. Don was right. I got a big static shock in cold blowing snow. The wreck was neatly deposited on a flatbed truck waiting on the roadside a few miles away and I returned to Nelson as a passenger in the 204B. I was also a bit of a wreck.

I was grounded, which meant I wasn't allowed to fly until a decision was made on my status with the company. The call came from Vancouver on Christmas Eve just before quitting time. I was fired.

It had been a bad year for Okanagan Helicopters. They'd wrecked more than half their sixty-five helicopters before my episode and the insurance company was screaming for blood. It ended up being my blood. I headed for home realizing that I'd forgotten to wish Don a Merry Christmas. On the way, I picked up a bottle of scotch and took a swig. As I entered my mobile home the kids came running up to me all excited.

"Daddy, Daddy," my son Jeff shouted. "Santa's coming tonight."

The Christmas tree lights were on and the usual Christmas cooking smells were everywhere. I decided to say nothing to anyone about the past day's events until after Boxing Day, and prodded myself into a holiday mood. I even laughed at the thought that this might be quite a long holiday.

On December 27th, I went to the Okanagan office attached to the front of the hanger. There was no one there and the office was like a cold

Jeff and Linda. My first two kids.

stranger. I packed up my few belongings from the desk that had been installed for me just a few months before and threw my key on Don's desk.

I opened the door to the unheated hanger and entered. The familiar
smells of gas and oil were like perfume to me. The Hiller 12E that I'd
learned to fly in sat quietly on its wheels. I opened the door and climbed
into the pilot's seat for the last time. Tears welled up in my eyes, but I
drove them back and left the hanger hurriedly. It would be embarrassing
if Don turned up. In the following months, I only went to the hanger once
to pick up my final pay cheque.

The Unemployment office in Nelson was only a few blocks away
and it was open. Once again I began the long process of looking for employment that didn't include flying. Many of the jobs that I'd looked for
previously were still there. I was on the short list for a BC Conservation
Officer and for a Federal Indian agent.

After a week of filling out applications, I knew I would soon find a great ground position for life. By now the employment officer I'd been assigned to and I had become great friends.

"Look, Hank, you need to get some sort of job to keep you busy till we find you a position," my employment officer suggested. He found one for me almost too quickly.

The Canadian Pacific Railroad needed a labourer at the rail yard just a few blocks from the employment office. I was hired at minimum wage. All I had to do was learn how to drive a wheelbarrow. Most of the men had worked here their whole lives.

"You need to buy the foreman a bottle on payday if you want to keep working here," one of the more experienced wheel barrowers told me as I picked up my first meagre cheque.

I never gave that foreman a bottle and I was never fired. All in all, it was a pretty crappy job, but it put food on the table. Day after day, I would see the new helicopter that had replaced the one that I'd wrecked, flying low over the rail yard that was right next to Okanagan's base.

Just after New Years, I was still dreaming that I might get another flying job. I sent out applications for employment to every helicopter company in western Canada. The few that answered said, "Unable to hire you due to your insurance status." This was their polite way of saying, "You're a high risk."

Two miserable months dragged by and the low CPR pay had us eating hamburger instead of steak. I was no closer to finding a decent job. I was out shovelling what I hoped was the last March snowfall when my wife called me to the phone. It was Jim Lapinski, chief pilot for Klondike Helicopters in Calgary.

"Why don't you come on over here? We'll talk and take a flight test.

Maybe I can offer you a job." We talked over the details and I hung up high as a kite with excitement. When I told Melba the glorious news she simply looked away.

I scrounged some time off from my CPR position and headed for Calgary. After introductions and some chit chat, Jim and I climbed into a Bell 47 G2 helicopter which was identical to the one I'd flown during the Okanagan Helicopters mountain course. I was a nervous wreck. Once airborne and clear of the airport Jim turned control of the helicopter over to me. Fear grabbed me! The controls felt like total strangers. My hands felt like frozen bear paws on an ice-covered tree. I managed to do everything reasonably well until he asked me to do an auto-rotation. All I could think about was that snowy creek in the bugaboos, hitting that invisible snag, that helicopter mortally wounded like a mosquito hit with a flyswatter, and me hurting.

I put the helicopter into auto-rotation, saw the ground roaring at me and froze. Jim grabbed the controls away from me just before we crashed. In mere seconds, we came to a skidding stop in a desolate prairie field and settled into snow-covered grain stubble.

A small pack of grey winter-gaunt coyotes took off in all directions. It was all over for me, I thought. Yet, at that terrible moment I realised I didn't want some boring ground job, I still wanted to fly.

Jim gently took my hand, placed it on the cyclic and said, "I know you can fly this thing, so let's do it. I'm getting thirsty for a beer and don't want to sit out here in the middle of nowhere all night. Now take off and climb to 500 feet."

After several long moments I finally opened the throttle and lifted the helicopter into a hover. Snow blew in all directions, but no trees were waiting in hiding to strike me down. I took off and climbed to 500 feet.

"Now I want you to auto-rotate right to the spot we just took off from," Jim said, suddenly closing the throttle.

We were instantly heading almost vertically towards the ground at 60 miles per hour. This time I flared the helicopter and did a perfect landing. I noticed that Jim's hands weren't far from the controls.

"You missed the spot by 50 feet," he said with a smile on his face. "Let's do better next time."

After several attempts, I was within ten feet.

"Not bad," Jim said smiling at me.

At last, I had my confidence back. The helicopter finally felt like it was part of me again. Jim was a sensitive and decent man who recognized that the last time I'd flown had ended up in a terrible accident. When we finally got back to the airport Jim lead me to his office, sat me down and said, "I have to go talk to the president about you."

Twenty long minutes later he came in and sat down quietly facing me. "We've called our insurance company and…."

He hesitated and I knew what was coming. My heart was pounding. This had been my last chance; the end of my flying career…. "We've decided to hire you. It's going to cost us a bundle for liability insurance, but I think you're worth the risk. Now let's go get that beer."

As we sat down for a celebratory beer, he said, "You were like a horse with a broken leg. A lot have to be put down, but some do survive."

With a new red Klondike hat on my head and on a decent salary, I phoned Melba from the motel that the company provided for the night.

I couldn't contain my excitement as I told her that I was once again a helicopter pilot, albeit on probation.

"Fine," was all she said and hung up on me. That was when I realized that our marriage was in trouble. I couldn't blame her. We'd been through hell since Christmas and she was quite tired of living with a helicopter pilot, especially one who was now going to be away for months on end. We sold the mobile home in Nelson and moved into an apartment in Calgary.

I'd been hired by Klondike with the title of Helicopter Pilot /Engineer, which gave the company the right to put me in coveralls. The closest I got to a helicopter for several months was with a paint stripper. My home life with Melba was pretty miserable.

"I'm leaving you," I finally told her.

She said some very bad things to me as I packed, but she and my two kids stood teary eyed at the door as I walked out for the last time.

On May 27, 1966, I put my car stuffed with my meagre belongings in storage. I headed for Fort Smith, capital of the Northwest Territories in a Bell 47 G2 for a three-month flying contract. It would be my first real test, as a helicopter pilot, once again. I remembered Lenny's old hackneyed flying expression, *"There are old pilots and bold pilots, but no old, bold pilots."* I'd been a bold pilot and had almost got myself killed. Now, I had a second chance to become an old pilot.

Helicopter Crash in the Bugaboos

A floundering beast buried deeply in the snow,
Gentle manipulation of each precise control,
Full power straining with the load,
Rotor blast a tornado by itself,
Thoughts of food and warmth just minutes off,
Takeoff slow then faster faster through the narrow draw,
A humming bird turned eagle after prey.

Crisp bugaboo cold and snow blue shadows,
Flickering light through wings
That move too fast to see,
An ice bound creek meandering below,
Receding fast beneath each tree,
A snag unseen ghostly hidden,
Reaching out with icy fingers,
To grasp this frail machine.

A metal rending crashing sound,
Sends this wondrous flying bird,
Unwilling into deathly throes,

To broken quiet metal.
Oh God, Will I ever try again!

Two men and I, bleeding bleeding,
Bitter cold, and wounds congealing,
Stiffening and aching bones,

The lifeblood sun too fast receding.

Three fearful men crawling through broken plexiglas,

Into neck-deep forbidding snow,

The dead bird machine, burning, burning

near snowbound men with nowhere left to go.

Will we be blown to peaceful forgiving eternity?

Warmed by the only fire left in this dead bird,

Or left to die in the arctic quiet this night.

Oh God, will I ever fly again?

Wrecked in the Bugaboos.

CHAPTER THREE

HENRY THE BUFFALO

"What were you doing up there?" I asked Bob Gauchie, who'd just gotten back from two weeks flying up in the Arctic. He was a Beaver pilot who was part of the team contracted to the Federal Department of Northern Affairs and Natural Resources for the summer. His welcome-back party was being held in the Fort Smith Royal Canadian Legion where Roger Sexty, a fellow helicopter pilot, and Bob and I felt it was our duty to keep the bartender employed and the beer in the taps from going flat. As usual, the Legion was almost empty.

Fort Smith was the capital of the Northwest Territories with a large mobile population of Federal civil servants, and a steady population of First Nations people.

"Spent two weeks flyin' from lake to lake with a geologist. Just him and me," Bob replied. "Tell you the truth I didn't know exactly where I was most of the time. Sure glad he didn't know that. There's thousands of lakes up there and they all look the same. Got home by sheer luck."

We all rolled our eyes. We knew Bob was exaggerating. The de Havilland Canada DHC-2 Beaver he flew was first built in 1948. It was a single-engine, high-wing, propeller-driven aircraft. Like its earlier relative the Norseman, it was one of the finest and most used bush planes in history. Though it was already classed as a short takeoff and landing aircraft, Bob managed to fly it into potholes even smaller than what it was designed for. Bob was a little more than 10 years older than me and had been a WWII veteran. We'd both learned to fly in the RCAF but our paths had never crossed. Now our paths not only crossed, but overlapped.

When wildfires happened Bob would fly the firefighters and equipment into the nearest lake and I would take them to the fire. I was still pretty new at this and Bob always had a hint or two to make things easier for me. This far north, it almost never got dark in the summer and we would often be airborne by 5 AM after a night of partying at the Legion. Even at that hour, he always managed a smile on his face, a joke in his mouth and a twinkle in his eye.

"So what's up with you guys?" Bob asked, sucking on another Legion beer.

"I'm going to herd buffalo tomorrow," I said as casually as possible, not wanting to sound like a boy who was about to take his first pee standing up.

"Didn't know you could ride a horse," Bob joked.

"These aren't cows we're looking at," Roger answered. "Buffalo can run a horse into the ground so choppers are the horse of choice. I've got another job tomorrow so it's Hank's turn to have a go."

Roger, who was sipping on a glass of wine instead of beer, was much older and more experienced than me. He was also quite a character, with the lean weathered look of a man from down under complete with Australian digger hat and uniform. The two of us were based in Fort Smith, which is right on the northeast edge of Wood Buffalo National Park. His primary job was working with the parks people and mine was forest fire fighting. Our jobs often overlapped, but this was my first crack at herding buffalo. I was sure it wouldn't be all that hard.

"You need fricken' chaps," Ernie Grant, our ever loving mechanic/ engineer, said with a big grin on his face when I arrived at the base early next morning.

His head was bald, except for a little hair trying to survive around his ears, and his eyes bulged white in contrast to his full dark beard. He probably shaved once a year just to check for food. He had my helicopter fuelled and ready to go. It sat on a rough lumber pad a comfortable distance away from Rogers's machine, which also sat on a rough hewn pad. We flew two almost identical Bell 47 G2 helicopters. These Bells had small, narrow cabins that could just about squeeze in two skinny passengers and a pilot, and then had hardly enough power to get off the ground even at this low altitude. Like most of the Bell 47s, this model trundled along at about 70 mph.

Our base was on a very picturesque grassy knoll above the mighty Slave River. I took off over the steep cliff and headed for Haycamp which was a half hour flight over the park. The boiling frothy rapids directly below had given Fort Smith its Chipewyan language name, *Thebacha*, which meant, *'beside the rapids.'* Just below the rapids, Bob's Beaver was docked beside other aircraft in the calmer water. The rapids quickly turned into a lazy, meandering river, which made its way through the 17,300 square miles of Wood Buffalo National Park straddling the border between the Northwest Territories and Alberta. The park, which was home to several thousand wood buffalo, moose, wolves, caribou, bears and many thousands of other smaller furry and feathery creatures, was also the last natural nesting ground for whooping cranes in the world. It was also home to about a thousand different species of mosquitoes and other annoying bugs.

Fifteen minutes into the flight, the landscape of sparse trees that popped up amongst seven-foot high grass turned into blue ponds dotted with thousands of water birds. The ponds were surrounded by green meadows and swamps. A lone moose stood with his head half submerged in a swamp, munching on underwater greenery. A pack of black and white wolves fed off a small dead animal. There were buffalo everywhere, mostly in groups of a few dozen or so. If I spotted a dead buffalo today, I would have to abandon my herding mission, fly back to Fort Smith, pick up a waiting biologist and return to the site as quickly as possible. He would perform an on-the-spot autopsy to see if anthrax or tuberculosis had caused the death. These two diseases were rampant in the park.

Haycamp appeared off in the distance. Miles and miles of strong fencing stretched forth in the shape of a huge V. Where it came together the parks people had built an enormous 10-foot-high log corral. Rough-hewn outbuildings scattered here and there were quarters for a crew of equally rough-hewn men.

Peter Miller, the Crew Chief, who was a biologist, stood by the helicopter pad holding his hat firmly atop his head so the rotor blast wouldn't blow it away. I landed and shut down beside dozens of fuel drums, that had been hauled in by truck in the winter, when the tundra was frozen rock solid. I topped up the two saddle fuel tanks, knowing I would need every drop. I also carried two ten-gallon kegs on the racks which meant I could fly about 4 hours before I would have to return here to refuel. I was sure the buffalo would appreciate the break.

My Bell 47 G2 fueled and ready to herd buffalo.

"So it's your turn to have a go at herding," Peter said as we shook hands. "Let's go have a coffee and I'll fill you in on your mission today."

We sat at a small table just outside the cook house overlooking the corral where about 50 buffalo pressed against the rough logs looking restless and jumpy.

Peter wasn't a big man, but he was solidly built with a wind-weathered face that looked both knowledgeable and intelligent. Pale grey eyes squinted at me in the sun.

"Yesterday, a cow carrying an unborn calf just kept running into the log fence over and over again until she broke her neck. Over the years, I've seen this happen many times. I don't know of any other wild animal that would do this. We tried to coax her away with treats, but to no avail," Peter said with a sad look in his eyes. "Everyone calls these park animals buffalo," he added, "but they were originally a Wood Bison, which is a larger and darker relative of the Plains Bison that populated the prairie grasslands by the millions a few hundred years ago."

As we sipped on our coffee, Peter went on to explain that the Wood Bison is also called a Mountain Buffalo and was the largest land animal in North America. They can reach over 9 feet in length, more than 6 feet tall and can weigh over a ton.

Peter further explained that in 1922 Wood Buffalo National Park was established to protect the herd. Shortly after that, about 6,000 Plains Bison were moved from southern Alberta to the park. Interbreeding virtually eliminated the Wood Bison as a separate species. In 1893, there were less than 500 animals left in the park when hunting them was finally prohibited. So by 1900, the number grew to about 1500 and quickly increased to a population over 10,000. Overgrazing and disease not only killed off thousands of them, but threatened the caribou and moose population as well.

"We've got a population of about 5,000 buffalo out there that need their TB shots. Unlike anthrax, tuberculosis is treatable with vaccine. We inoculate the young ones and the unlucky, older guys are butchered for meat which, in my opinion, is really only edible as jerky. Get yourself another coffee while I go and get you a map of the area," Peter said and trundled off.

I filled my cup from the dented pot that sat on the equally bent woodstove. A huge pan of cold bacon left over from breakfast sat next to coffee pot. I was back at the table munching on some of it, when Peter returned with a full coffee cup and an old crinkled map that looked like a few buffalo had walked on it.

"Roger and I did some scouting yesterday. There's several hundred buffalo scattered in the trees in this area," he said, circling the location on the map which was about 10 miles south of our location. If you're lucky you might get some in the corral by nightfall. Fly on down there and see what you can do."

I took off and headed south. Even this early in the morning the sun was well up and hot. Soon, I saw mixed groups of buffalo gathering in the shade of birch and alder trees, or wallowing in the cool mud of swamps. I sped towards the herd, hovering so close, they could feel the wash from the blades. I made slow wide circles much like a cowboy on horseback would do, only going close enough to scare them into moving. Things went smooth as silk. In 40 minutes, I had close to 500 animals assembled together exactly where I wanted them. The bulls glared and snorted at me and raised dust with their hooves while the cows sheltered their young calves.

"This is a cinch," I said to myself as I hovered above them thinking about the thousands of cowboys and proud Indians riding on lathered horses who must have taken days to accomplish what I had done in minutes. All that I was missing was the roar of hundreds of restless hoofs, which were drowned out by my engine. I hovered in close to the largest group fully expecting them to obediently head north where the corral waited. Not one buffalo moved. They simply shuffled around like a bunch of nervous school boys at a junior high school dance.

"Oh, oh," I said to myself. "Maybe this isn't going to be as easy as I thought."

It was then that I noticed a huge bull off by himself, standing dead still but for a hoof gently scuffing at the ground. He was much bigger and darker than the rest and I wondered, "Could this be the last pure Wood Bison that Peter had said was all but extinct in the park?"

I moved in close to him. As the windblast ruffled his black mane, he simply stared at me with a defiant gleam in his eye. His mouth was moving and I imagined him saying, "I'll move when I'm good and ready," although he was probably just chewing a bit of grass.

"OK, Henry," I shouted using my childhood name, "when you get tired of eating dust, you'll move."

I remembered my Uncle Henry who I was named after. He died flying a Spitfire in the Battle of Britain. "You're as determined and stubborn as your uncle and all those brave men who fought in the Battle of Britain and saved a nation," my English father used to say when I was young. He came from Yorkshire, England, in the 1920s.

It was as if Henry The Buffalo had read my thoughts. He gave me a beady annoyed look and trotted off north. The whole herd followed, leaving me tagging along. By noon I'd only managed to get about half the herd to the fenceline leading into the corral. Henry would lead a group of fifty into those blasted copses of trees and four would run out the other side.

"You aren't going to wear my chaps out." I shouted, more determined than ever to get some of them into the corral. Towards the end of the day, close to 500 buffalo had dissolved into the canopy of trees. Henry was the only one left. Now he was running next to the fence and I had him trapped. The miles of V-shaped fence gradually closed in. Men were waiting at the gate ready to lock him in the corral. I remembered Peter's chilling words. All the old buffalo would go to the meat processing plant. Henry suddenly came to an abrupt halt, turned and stared at me.

"I'm going to get you in that corral before nightfall and they're going to make you into hamburger," I shouted hovering in so close that we were virtually face to face.

The wind, the noise, and my smug face seemed to bother him now. Drool dripped from his mouth, lather and sweat had left a sheen on his dark body. Now, I saw exhaustion in his face and he was shaking uncontrollably. I'd been flying for almost eight hours and had been pushing this solitary animal for most of it. He must have been as tired of running as I was of sitting. I was every bit as sore in the saddle as the old Texan cowboys must have been and no doubt Henry hurt more. The heat from the July sun and the dust from hundreds of hooves had left me feeling like a sweating mud pie.

Suddenly, he turned and darted into a large patch of trees.

"You sneaky old bugger," I said laughing, in spite of my annoyance. "Come out and fight face-to-face." I circled the large grove, but there was no sign of him.

We both needed a break so I landed beside a crystal blue pond a short distance away and shut down. That big bull wasn't going anywhere. The rotor slowly came to a stop. A waft of wind rustled the tall grass and rippled the pond. Water lapped musically against the gravely shoreline. The rotor thumped rhythmically on the mast. Geese honked and ducks quacked at me from a safe distance. I dragged what was left of my sandwiches from my lunch box and munched on them. Mallards saw the bread I threw on the ground and moved closer. Even though it was suppertime, the Sun was still high on the horizon and it was hot. Condensation dripped from the canvas water bag hanging on the skid. I gulped down large mouthfuls of water and poured some on my head to try to cool down. Then it occurred to me that I was sitting right beside a swimming pool and I sure didn't need a bathing suit out here. I stripped naked and jumped into the pond. The water was deep and cold and soon revitalized me. I swam towards the ducks, sending them noisily into flight. I'd done a fair bit of skinny dipping in my life, even shared it with a female companion, but it had never felt as good as this. Within a few short minutes I heard a snort behind me. I gasped out loud and almost choked on a mouthful of water as I turned back towards shore. There, standing dangerously close to the helicopter, was Henry sucking up water from the pond. I treaded water trying not to make waves. Fear gripped me, making goose bumps from the cold water stand out even more.

No longer did I have the power of the helicopter behind me. It was now a 2000-pound animal against a 160-pound skinny dipper.

After drinking his fill, Henry rolled around in the mud a few times. Then, with a quick almost placid look back at me, he trotted off and began chewing on the lush grass close to the lake. I swam to shore and sat in the helicopter naked with the doors open until the wind and heat dried me. Then I got dressed and prepared to start up the helicopter. The moment I hit the starter, Henry jumped like he'd been hit with a cattle prod. He turned towards me glaring and pawing the ground.

We were both refreshed and ready to do battle. I closed in on Henry once more, but this time I chased him away from the corral and out of the big V-shaped fencing. I was not prepared to see this brave magnificent beast turned into hamburger. It only took a gentle nudging as he was quite willing to go. The only eyewitnesses were the ducks who'd returned to the lake. As I flew back to Fort Smith, the setting sun was a blaze of orange and turquoise fading to purple. Reflections off the numerous ponds looked like glistening gemstones.

The next day Roger was back at work with the buffalo and I flew a biologist back into the park to check on the whooping cranes.

"Hey, great work, mate," Roger said that night as we sat once again in the Legion. "You did a terrific job. I got most of the herd in the corral today; all except one old bull. They've been trying to catch him for years. He's one big bugger, aye."

"He is and he's also smart. Bet you four pints that they never catch him," I replied. "And by the way, I named him Henry!"

CHAPTER FOUR

THOSE AMAZING WHOOPING CRANES

"I need a helicopter on floats," Mark, one of the parks biologists, had said on the phone. "We're going to visit the Whooping Cranes."

"Hope you're not landing in freakin' deep water," Ernie said, doubtfully, as he stared at the two blobs of black rubber hidden behind our small shed, which turned out to be a ratty set of helicopter floats. He worked late into the night patching, inflating and installing them on the helicopter. When I arrived in the morning, the helicopter was ready to go. It looked a lot less sleek with those big, ugly, patched up floats under her.

"Had to wear a paint mask," he said dolefully in the morning, "so I wouldn't inhale the clouds of flippin' no-see-ums."

Mark arrived in rubber chest waders, with an array of equipment. I tied all his equipment on the rack and off we went. As we headed to one of the nesting areas marked with a big X on his map, a montage of muskeg, meandering streams, shallow lakes, bogs and huge beaver ponds passed under us. Small patches of dry forest comprised of Spruce, Jack pine, and a large variety of shrubs dotted the area as well and were the reason I was on contract up here. Fire is a natural force in this area. During the 20-minute flight, Mark gave me a crash course on Whooping Cranes.

"In 1860 there were about 1400 in North America," Mark shouted over the ever-whining helicopter engine. "Our good old settlers started popping them off for their fine feathers and meat or for target practice. By 1912, there were about a hundred left, which probably would have dropped to zero if they hadn't been put on the protected list. In the forties, the protected Cranes dropped to a population of about sixteen. Right now our situation isn't much better.

"It's too early in the year for exact statistics, but that's what this trip is all about. We're going to land in the pond a safe distance from the Cranes and I'm going check to see if there are any eggs or chicks in the nest," he added. "They usually lay two."

By this time we were circling over a large swampy pond that had a gun-blue glint to it.

"That nest is about three feet across," Mark shouted pointing to the single nest just about dead in the middle, "and it's probably made of bulrushes and cattails. They're the largest bird in North America and this pair stand at least five feet tall."

Mommy Crane sat hopefully on her eggs. Daddy Crane stood in about a foot of water on long black legs, dipped his head into the water and came out with a frog in his mouth.

"They're mainly meat eaters," he added, "but they also eat roots and water plants."

They had long white necks and huge white bodies, except for the black feathers on the tips of their wings. Characteristic red patches on their heads contrasted with their long black beaks, with a touch of bristly black on either side. You could tell they weren't happy about us being there. By the time we'd circled a couple of times looking for a place to land, they were doing what looked like a mad hatter dance, bowing their heads, flapping their wings and glaring at us with bright yellow eyes.

After circling several times, I finally found an open patch of muskeg on the edge of the pond just large enough that the rotors would be clear of the trees.

I landed and firmly imbedded the floats in the muck, hoping they weren't leaking. I shut down the helicopter.

I had floats so why not just land in the water? Two reasons: unlike float planes with keels and rudders, even the mildest wind would send the helicopter skittering into the trees before the rotor stopped. Second, on start up the helicopter will turn 180 to 360 degrees before the tail rotor does its job of controlling the torque of the main rotor. It's a great way to remove the tail rotor in the trees.

"Enjoy the show," Mark said. He collected his equipment and headed for the Cranes. The ankle deep water rose higher and higher up his chest waders, threatening to overflow into his underwear. It shallowed out near the nest. I'd had no idea how huge these birds were until Mark got close to them. They stood side by side at full height ready to do battle, making Mark looking like David standing up to Goliath. Then they both spread their six-foot wings creating what looked like a protected impregnable approach to the nest. If I had been me out there I would have preferred to be dressed in body armour.

These tall birds squawked and made a strange whooping sound, which was probably how they got their name. They thrashed at poor Mark as he valiantly waded around them and peeked into their nest. Then, they chased him right back to the helicopter beating at him with their wings and pecking at his back.

"Two eggs in the nest ready to hatch," Mark shouted at me over the squawking birds. "Let's get the heck outa here!"

I pushed the starter button, hoping that the rapidly accelerating rotors wouldn't cause trouble for these magnificent birds.

By the time we took off and headed for Fort Smith, the Whoopers had already gone full bore back to their nest. The rotor blast hardly ruffled their feathers.

Mark and I made several more trips that summer to different Whooping Crane nests, carefully recording their egg production. At that time research was an ongoing perennial program.

Two years later, early in June, Jim Lapinski met me as I landed in Calgary with the company's first Jet Ranger. I had been flying most of the winter and both the helicopter and I needed some time off. As we walked towards the office, Jim gave me that hang dog look of his which meant he wanted something and he wasted no time telling me.

"Look, Hank," he said, "I know you want some time off, but I need a favour. It'll just take one day."

I shot him a sour look, but my curiosity got the better of me.

"What?" I said.

"Well, we got a call from Ernie Kuyt, a park biologist up in Fort Smith. He wants to do a Whooping Crane survey and needs someone who knows the area. That means you or Roger, but he's off on another job."

"OK," I replied, "what time's my flight booked out?"

"Well ah… there's a G2 helicopter sitting here ready to go," Jim replied, looking a little sheepish.

"A one-day job! It's a 10-hour flight to Fort Smith!" I exclaimed.

"Well, how about you leave the helicopter there and fly back commercially? I'll get someone else to pick it up. Pay raises come up in month," he added winking. "What do you think?"

I took the bribe and took off next morning for Fort Smith. Once again I was flying the old G2 helicopter and it was kind of fun. It was really only used for training now, but the slowness of the helicopter was relaxing and reminded me of what an airline pilot friend told me.

"Hell, on days off I fly an old Tiger Moth to get sane again!"

The next day Ernie Kuyt and I did a five-hour Whooping Crane survey in the park without landing. Ernie wasn't just a biologist – to these Cranes he was more like a mother hen with a bunch of chicks. He had special names for all of them.

"That's Sally over there," he said pointing to a Whooping Crane that was fiddling at her nest with her long neck and beak. She rules that roost."

Between the two of us we identified and recorded most of the nests. During the flight he told me of his plans to save the Whooping Cranes.

"As you already know Whooping Cranes usually lay two eggs. We've now learned that most of the time one chick dies. I've sold everyone on the idea that, if we take one egg and incubate it, we just might save a chick's life and save a bird headed for extinction," Ernie shouted over the engine noise. "Once safely in Fort Smith the egg is shipped by jet to Ottawa then to Washington for incubation. We have no way of knowing if the egg left behind will survive, but we are confident that the egg we ship will have a very good chance of survival."

I was to learn later that his strategy was one of the primary reasons that we still have Whooping Cranes today on this planet. I'm proud to this day that I had a small part in it.

That evening Ernie and I landed at the deserted heliport in Fort Smith.

"Good luck with the Whoopers," I said to Ernie as we shook hands.

I watched him as he walked towards the Department of Northern Affairs panabode office, a short distance away from the heliport. Just about everything to do with the park was run from this small building. Ernie suddenly knelt and plucked a few weeds from the fast-growing garden the employees had planted. I felt that the Whooping Cranes were in good hands.

A gentle breeze seemed to carry the sound of the rapids closer. Off in the distance a Beaver aircraft was heading in to land in the still waters below the rapids. I was scheduled to catch the evening flight to Calgary so had a few hours to look around. I wondered if the Legion was still open. I walked the short distance swatting at clouds of mosquitoes. Young half-naked children played and squealed at one another, oblivious of the mosquitoes that covered their dark skin. An old man waved and grinned showing broken teeth. I remembered seeing him at one of the many fires I'd worked on here two years before.

The Legion was still open, but I wondered for how long. Fort Smith had lost its title as the official territorial capital to Yellowknife and the majority of its government employees had moved there.

A few old veterans that I remembered from two years ago were sitting at the same table. They waved me over and after re-acquainting ourselves one of them said, "Did you hear about Bob Gauchie?"

"Sure did," I replied.

At the end of the summer we'd both gone our separate ways and I never saw him again, but I sure did hear about him. He had made headlines the following winter when he was forced to land his Beaver on a small lake near the eastern shore of Great Bear Lake on Feb 3rd, 1967. He'd run into bad weather and this time he was really lost and out of fuel too. He'd survived for 58 days and was near death when they found him.

Bob and I had sat for many hours at this very table telling jokes, talking about our daily flights and RCAF adventures. I haven't the slightest doubt that if he were sitting here at this very moment with a mug of beer in his hand he would have said, "Two things kept me alive; I had four sleeping bags and a couple of boxes of frozen fish. Woulda traded all those fish for a case of beer and died with a smile on my face."

It wasn't just the fish and sleeping bags that saved him. Bob was another one of those true diehard Canadian bush pilots. These hard working, determined, good-natured pilots have made the Canadian North the great region it is today.

CHAPTER FIVE

MESSAGE IN A BOTTLE

"Hey, Hank," the dispatcher said, "we've got a forest fire up near Fort Resolution and we need you up there as soon as possible."

It was August 22nd, a day after my birthday. I had been painfully woken up by the irritating ringing of the telephone.

We took off from Fort Smith with the early morning sun at my back, or I should say we *barely* took off. Stuffed into the small cabin with me was Dick, a big burly trapper who would be in charge of the fire, and my oversized mechanic friend, Ernie, who would look after the helicopter. We followed the Slave River toward the small village of Fort Resolution. Moose browsed its banks and in one vast meadow buffalo walked over the bones of relatives caught in a winter kill.

A group of thirty Dene and Métis firefighters stood at the edge of the village waiting for us. Many of the older men were dressed in traditional buckskin, but the younger generation looked like they'd come straight out of a Hudson's Bay Store. One thing I knew for sure, in a week they'd

The forest fire on day one at Fort Resolution.

all look as raggedy as street bums. The forest fire was on the eastern shore of Great Slave Lake very close to Fort Resolution, one of the oldest established communities in the Northwest Territories.

Tents, sleeping bags, pick axes, shovels, food and weather-beaten personal packsacks were piled up like cordwood waiting to be hauled out to the fire.

We were on our own. Unless the fire got dangerously close and threatened to burn the village townsite to the ground, no water bombers or other helicopters would be sent.

I dropped Ernie off at the village to organize the fuel needed for the helicopter and lodging for us, then headed for the wildfire with Dick to have a look see.

"She's a dooser," Dick shouted at me as we flew into the gut wrenching turbulence generated by the wind-whipped flames. Large evergreen trees torched up by the rapidly-expanding fire quickly turned into blackened twigs. Terrified moose, deer and smaller animals ran for their lives. Some weren't fast enough and were burned to a crisp. Other creatures jumped into small lakes and swamps. The black soot-filled smoke would probably kill them. We circled the fire and Dick calmly planned where he was going to put the fire camps. They had to be close enough for the crew to fight the fire, but not so close that the fire would burn them out.

"We'll put a camp here, another there, and one by that lake," he told me pointing. "Let's go do it."

It took me the rest of the day to place the men and transport the equipment to Dick's scattered locations around the fire. Fifteen trips to get the men out and a dozen more to sling out the gear. The first day was hell. The government frumps in Fort Smith had forgotten a few minor details. No airplanes arrived that day with food.

"This is typical," Dick said matter of factly. "We'll take Simon Joe out and kill a moose." There were moose everywhere. No one was particularly worried about the totally illegal hunting of a moose from a helicopter.

Simon Joe was old, wrinkled, wiry and tough. It took him almost no time to locate and shoot one. Then he gutted the moose with the smooth skill of a surgeon, but before he did this he poked the animal's eyes out.

"Why'd he do that?" I asked Dick.

"So that the moose won't be able to chase him when they meet in the happy hunting ground," he replied with a grin.

The moose was too heavy to sling to the camp in one piece so we cut

Simon Joe with food for the fire camp.

it in two. By the time I arrived at the base camp with the second half, the natives had already cut up the first half. Huge slabs of fat hung over the campfire. The smoked fat would be eaten within hours. The meat would be boiled in fire-blackened pots for later.

At the end of the day, I plunked the helicopter on the pad that Ernie had roughed together. The chopper's inside smelled of sweat and raw-hide. The exterior was covered in ashes, soot, mud and dust.

Ernie stated his time-honoured opinion on it. "You've buggered my baby this time."

The winds twisted constantly, sending the snakelike flames in every direction. I moved smoky, sweaty men to new safe locations. They dug trenches only to have the quirky fire turn and send them running for their lives. Men with backpacks full of water pumped away at hot spots with little effect. I flew from dawn to dusk, ate on the run, and fell into bed exhausted right after supper. Ernie worked well into each night. Bugs and ashes that clung to the rotors like ice had to be scraped off.

The plexiglas bubble had to be washed and polished each night so I could see out the next day. And at least twenty gritty bearings needed to be pumped regularly with copious quantities of clean grease.

September snuck in cold and frosty. The fire no longer sizzled. The flames subsided to little more than few dozen scattered brushfires looking like Boy Scout camp fires. But it burned quietly, deep in the muskeg.

Trees keeled over like dominos in its slow, moving path. Soon even that relentless fire would be killed by forty below weather which would freeze the muskeg down several feet. Now the men had a fighting chance. New fire trenches were dug into the cold ground. Hand-held water pumps killed the flames one by one. The 8 to 10-hour flying days were now down to a fun level of 3 to 4 hours per day.

The three of us who stayed in the village were bedded down in the old St. Joseph's Catholic Mission, an enormous multi-storey, turn-of-the-century residential school whose lone resident was the town's priest. Richly panelled walls blended with very creaky and well worn floors. There was no running water, but each room had an antique glass wash-bowl and pitcher.

The priest who lived in a little suite on the main floor ran the unused residence as if it was still bubbling with children. He was a small frail-looking man, but he had the will and drive of a lion. He made no bones about how absolutely delighted he was to have us here. We lived two floors up, each with our own room.

"Sorry there's no shower for you fellas," the old man said. "Can't seem to get it running. Sometimes, if you bang on the pipes, it works."

Ernie Grant, my ever-vigilant engineer, took on the task of getting us a working shower. This big bear of a man never failed to amaze me. He banged around so much that the dust came unsettled in the building. After two days of noisy fiddling he proudly announced: "Got the freaker going! All you hafta do is bang the pipe three times and turn on the water."

Then he turned to me and whispered, "If this place ain't haunted then I'm a shrieken' swordfish."

We all quietly agreed with Ernie. Strange noises and footsteps in the night made one think there just might be some other 'not so living' in this old building.

Needless to say, the old priest developed a real fondness for Ernie. Now that things had slowed for him in the helicopter maintenance department, Ernie turned his restless energy into having the old building running like a four star hotel. He even polished up the beautiful antique washbowls and pitchers in every room. Ernie was one of those rare sorts who was equally at home in coveralls covered in motor grease or a chef's apron covered in more edible fare.

John LaPoint was the area resident fire warden, and one of just a few white men living in the village. He lived in one of the well-kept houses in the village, so close to the helicopter pad that the rotor blast shook the shakes on the roof and dusted up the windows He was a jovial, good natured French Canadian with a twinkle in his eye and a mouthful of jokes. His wife, Simone, cooked meals for the three of us when we weren't eating out at the camps. There was no hotel or restaurant in the town.

We were all drinking John's homemade wine, when a very lovely girl came to visit his wife, who was in the kitchen cleaning up. I peeked just a little.

"Who's that girl?" I asked John.

"Dat's Michelle," John replied grinning, "She works at de hospital. Bright girl dat one. 'Ard to get to know though, very quiet, but ain't she a beauty."

"Michelle," he shouted from the front room. "Come 'ere, meet 'Ank."

"'Ank 'ere's the helicopter pilot on the fire. He's bin' peekin' at you," he added as Michelle entered the front room with a dirty plate in her hand. She simply wrinkled her nose cutely and laughed at John's brashness. I squirmed and stopped breathing.

Her natural outdoorsy beauty filled the room. Old blue jeans and a man's shirt couldn't hide her lithe figure. She wore no makeup or jewellery. Striking olive skin and long black hair enhanced her remark-able walnut-coloured eyes.

I got a smile, a quick "Hi" and she was gone, back to the kitchen. We carried on with our little party and I didn't notice her leave.

It was dusk when I set out to walk the short distance to the mission. Pungent smoke drifting from the fire hung like a London fog over the whole village. An old woman pulling a rickety cart loaded with firewood passed me. A Mountie nodded a greeting towards me as he did his rounds. He would be looking for illegal firewater, no doubt. Alcoholic beverages were forbidden in this town. The RCMP enforced this with an iron fist. I don't know who made the law, but the joke was on them. Everyone made their own home brew and drank it quietly behind curtained windows in the dark.

The only real sign of life was the Community Centre. As I passed by it I heard the lively sounds of teenagers inside. Elvis's music blared in the background.

"Hi," a woman's voice said softly behind me. I nearly jumped out of my skin.

The women in this village seemed to be very shy. Not one had ever spoken to me on the street before. I turned in shocked surprise and there stood Michelle.

"Oh, hi there," was the best I could muster up.

We stood in awkward silence for a moment. Then she broke the ice by wrinkling that nose again and laughing at our awkwardness. I wondered, *was this really an accidental meeting?*

"Would you like to see our community hall?" she asked in such an easy way that I felt like had known her for years.

"Sure," I replied and followed her like a tap dancing rooster.

The place was bursting with life. Several teenagers twisted and turned on the dance floor trying to keep up with the Elvis song that scratched on an old record player. They snuck looks at the two of us whispering and laughing in a conspiratorial manner, but they all seemed very comfortable with my presence. Perhaps it was because I was with Michelle. The small concession stand had a choice of pop, chocolate bars and chips. I bought Michelle an Orange Crush and I had a Coke.

We sat together on a hard wooden bench watching a large group of kids who sat around a table playing Monopoly. I could easily have joined them.

Michelle accepted my invitation to walk her home. She lived at the edge of town at the end of a long row of ramshackle old houses that didn't look fit enough to last the winter. The roads were dirt and there were no sidewalks. At an opening between two houses a dozen mangy, half-starved dogs were tied to separate posts with cheap rope that looked too weak to hold Toy Terriers. As we drew close they growled and tugged fiercely at that fragile twine. Their eyes burned into us and razor sharp teeth glistened with drool.

Michelle grabbed my hand and pulled me away quickly.

"They don't know you and would probably tear you to pieces if they broke free. They're sled dogs and are only useful in the winter. In summer the owner feeds them just enough to keep them alive. I'm safe with them because I feed them the leftover fish that my father catches."

"I've decided that I'm going to take another route home for sure. The expression 'chained up' doesn't seem to apply here," I shakily replied.

Michelle laughed at this and I was thrilled to realize that she wasn't letting go of my hand.

As we stood clumsily at her front door I did what all red blooded helicopter pilots would do. I offered to take her for a helicopter ride the next day. She accepted and I headed back to the Mission, avoiding those dogs.

"Hey great," Dick shouted over the engine roar as we did our morning rounds, "Bring her out to the camp for lunch."

Michelle was waiting with Ernie when I landed at the village. I could tell he had her well-trained on helicopter safety. She wore a company cap which she clung to tightly as the rotor blast hit her. There's no shade in a helicopter bubble so hats come in handy. She crouched low as he led her to the helicopter, helped her inside and secured her seat belt. As I slowly lifted off the ground and tipped it into forward flight, she looked at me with the only fear I would ever see from her. We rose higher and higher and the fear on her face turned into astonishment.

"There's where my father's boat is and that's the house I was born in. Oh, look at the fire."

Words of wonder and excitement came one after the other. Gone was the quiet matter-of-fact girl.

And the looks she gave me as I skilfully manoeuvred the helicopter in any direction she wanted to go sent my ego on a spree. We flew over the smouldering fire and she waved frantically at the men working below. Her knuckles turned a little white as I hovered into the high trees that surrounded the base camp. We landed on the pad beside the cook tent. I shut down and helped her out of the helicopter. Dick waved us toward the cook tent. Decent food had at last arrived from Fort Smith. Smoked moose fat was not on the menu. The forest fire was all but forgotten. On our return to the village John met us at the helicopter pad.

"'Ow do you like flying, Michelle? You like it? I want you to come to supper tonight at my place, if dat's alright with you," he said.

My heart skipped a beat or two as she mulled this over and finally said, "Yes, I would like that, John."

After the feast, we guys sat uncomfortably with over-stuffed gullets at the dining room table drinking more of John's illegal home brew. Ernie had snuck in on us, always a welcome guest. We talked about the history of Fort Resolution and about the people who lived here. Michelle and Simone chatted in the kitchen and fussed over dirty dishes.

"Hey, 'Ank, why don't ya take Michelle out to the old ruins on Great Slave Lake. Ya wanna see the land marks around 'ere dat's one of the best. Over a hundred years old. You can take my car," John said.

Without waiting for a reply John was off to the kitchen and I heard him say, "Aye, Michelle, you wanna show 'Ank the old ruins?"

"Sure," she replied.

"I've got fricken maintenance on the chopper till near noon tomorrow," Ernie said with a wink. "Just don't get lost out there."

John had one of the few cars in the village, if that's what you call an old Buick with a questionable life expectancy, but it moved once you got it started.

There was no year-round road out of this village. Only in the winter once everything was frozen solid were roads built on the frozen lakes and tundra. They were called ice roads and trucks travelled on them twenty four hours a day bringing needed supplies to these isolated villages.

The ruins were on the tip of a peninsula on Resolution Bay. The five miles of road was twisty but firm and gravely until just before the ruins. There it dipped into notorious tundra mud. And that's where we got stuck!

"Sorry, Michelle. Now how the heck are we going to get home?" I asked, upset at the predicament I'd gotten us into. "What's John going to say?"

Michelle just stared, giggled, and said, "I guess we walk. Now let's go look at the ruins."

We crawled over old crumbling hand-carved stones and stared at weather-beaten monuments. She told me things about the past. We were easy together. Later we walked down the deserted beach hand-in-hand talking about my flying and her life in the village. It had been a glorious warm September day and now the sun was setting across the vast expanse of Great Slave Lake. Michelle pointed to a bay off in the distance backed by two mountainous humps that the sun was setting between and giggled.

"That's Sulphur Bay," she said laughingly. "I have seen an 1820 map that calls it 'Breasts like a Woman Bay,' probably named by my people. Do you think the oil companies had anything to do with the change?"

It was my turn to laugh.

It was growing cold. The dew was settling and beginning to harden. The bugs were gone, and the leaves were beginning to turn, gold plating the summer greenness.

"What's it like where you live?" she asked.

"Well, back home in Calgary they're still plucking potatoes from the warm ground," I replied. "Let's light a fire."

We sat on a log, and watched the sun sinking over the bay. She drew close and I kissed her. In this lonely historic place huge wonderful passion was building in me.

But as the sky turned a brilliant red then faded slowly to purple, Michele became distant and moved away from me.

"I'll probably die here!" she suddenly blurted out staring at me with pleading shackled eyes. Then she jumped up and walked away down the beach in the fading light. I sat on the log, stunned, not knowing what to do. I put more wood on the fire and waited, wondering if she was walking the five miles to the village. I walked to the car and tried to get it out of the wretched mud. It only sunk in deeper. I returned to the fire and poked at it.

Michelle appeared out of the darkness, sat beside me and took my hand. We sat quietly for a while just holding hands and then she said, "When I was a little girl we used to come out here to swim and picnic. I thought Great Slave Lake was the biggest lake in the world. I threw a bottle in the water with my name and address in it thinking it would go to some exotic land where someone would pick it up and write to me."

I looked at my watch. It was long past midnight.

"We'd better go," I said.

We walked along the crooked road hand in hand, with the moon blinking through the trees just enough to show us the way. The miles slipped by easily. I did most of the talking and she just listened. Finally, we walked over a rise in the road and saw the moonlit village growing closer with every step.

"Come this way," she said, leading me off the road on a narrow darkened trail that soon widened into the primitive runway that edged on the village.

"This is my favourite place," she said. "I watch the planes take off and think about going with them. One day I will. I'll walk the beaches of California and Hawaii where it's wild and deserted and once again throw another bottle into the water and watch it float out to sea. This time there'll be more than just my name in it. I'll write about who I am and where I live and about what it's like to live in a northern village. Is this a crazy thought?"

"It's a wonderful thought, "I replied. "When I was young I lived right on the ocean. I loved to walk the beaches and pick up the little crabs that hid under the rocks."

"Oh, there's the Big Dipper," she suddenly exclaimed, pulling me down on a thick soft patch of moss. "See how the two stars on the end of the bowl point to the North Star."

We lay side by side staring up at the brilliant northern sky.

"The North Star reminds me of Fort Resolution," she said sadly. "It stays still and the world moves around it."

She moved close and kissed me. Suddenly, the sled dogs began to bark un-controllably. Something moved in the bushes startling us and bringing me back to reality. Michelle shivered from the cold.

We walked hand in hand through the quiet village to her home. My parting words as she entered the darkened house were, "I really like you, Michelle, and I want to see you tomorrow night."

"We'll see," she replied. Then she hugged me, kissed me gently on the cheek and quickly went inside.

As I walked toward the old mission my feeling of fiery euphoria cooled as I remembered Michelle's last two words. But I knew I'd see her somehow.

It was noon the next day when I heard another helicopter approaching.

Ernie was up greasing the rotor head and as always I was chattering away. The other helicopter landed beside us, shut down and Charley Gibbons, one of the company pilots, jumped out with a big smile on his mug. He couldn't wait to tell me the good news.

"Hank," he said, "you're relieved. You're supposed to take the helicopter to Fort Smith right away. They've got reservations for you tomorrow for Calgary. You're due for time off."

My first thought was relief. I needed a break. It had been a long summer. Then I remembered last night. I wanted to growl like those sled dogs and say, "Bugger off," but poor Charley didn't deserve that. I had to see Michelle. I left Charley standing there and headed for her house kicking up a trail of dust.

It was a Saturday. Michelle's mother answered the door.

"Michelle's gone fishing with her Dad out on the lake and won't be back until late," she told me.

I walked to the mission to pick up my things, feeling pretty distraught. The old priest met me at the door. I told him I had to leave.

"I know, I heard," he said. "I want to talk to you."

We walked into his dusty little office and he ushered me into a tattered old chair. The walls were covered with old black and white pictures that told the history of a young priest living and growing old in this amazing village.

"You have made a good impression on these people;" he said kindly. "Michelle has talked to me. We are very close. Now I must tell you what I told her. It would be best if you left her with her people and in my care."

We sat quietly for a while, the only sound being the *tick-tock* of an old hand-carved wind-up clock that hung haphazardly on the wall. Finally, we shook hands and he ushered me out of his office. I climbed up the creaky stairs for the last time, walked down the haunted hallway and collected my belongings. Heavy with packsack and emotion I walked over to John and Simone's house and said my goodbyes, then walked the short distance to the helicopter. Dick and Charley had already taken off for the fire.

As I climbed aboard the helicopter, Ernie said, "Gonna miss ya," and batted me gently on the arm. Before heading for Fort Smith I flew along the road that Michelle and I had walked and flew a circle around the ruins where we had explored. The old Buick still sat in the mud waiting to be rescued. Great Slave Lake was smooth as glass except where several fish boats created pencilled lines across its surface.

I knew that Michelle was in one of them. Then I took one last look at the forest fire site. The flames had died. All that was left of the once-raging fire were smouldering embers.

CHAPTER SIX

THE MOIL FOR GOLD

"Ya wanna beer, you gotta buy a sandwich," the overworked waitress said over and over again to all the new arrivals. Beer was all they served, and you had to buy a cheese sandwich for 25 cents if you wanted a bottle of it. If you wanted another round, you hung on to that sandwich for dear life. Turn your back or go for a pee and the sandwich was whisked away and sold to the next beer drinker for the same sum.

"Came up with the idea to outfox those old Yukon bible punchers around here," Al Kulan said, "who passed a law saying you had to have a meal if you wanted to drink alcohol. Hell, in Whitehorse the stylish bars and dance halls are open 24 hours a day and nobody's interested in eating."

Al owned the trailer that served as the only restaurant in Ross River. Attached to the restaurant by a series of rough hewn boardwalks that criss-crossed haphazardly over a muddy patch of land was Al Kulan's hotel. It was really nothing more than a hastily assembled group of trailers on the edge of Ross River, an old Native village about 130 miles north-east of Whitehorse. Each trailer was divided into small sparsely-furnished rooms with two metal cots. I was lucky to have a room to myself, as most had to share.

The town of Ross River stood at the junction of the Ross and Pelly rivers. It was always a major stop-off for travellers coming north from the Upper Liard River and those travelling east over the mountains to points on the Mackenzie River. The area served as a gathering place for Native peoples who would congregate here in the late summer. It was first described by Robert Campbell, a Hudson's Bay Company pioneer, who visited the area in the summer of 1843, and named both rivers. A permanent settlement was begun in the summer of 1901 by Tom Smith, who set up a fishing camp. Most of the townspeople were members of the Dena tribe.

Jim Lapinsky phoned me a week earlier in my motel room in Calgary, where I had been visiting with my kids, and said, "How'd you like to go to Whitehorse for a month or two to relieve one of the base pilots?"

During the previous two weeks I had been miserable. I was moping over the loss of Michelle, who I'd left in Fort Resolution, and I was quite happy to escape the city that I jokingly called a "chrome-plated cow town." Where else in the world would you see rich oil men in white shirts and ties one day and the next day dressed in cowboy hats and fancy engraved boots? My kids weren't happy about me leaving them behind once again.

I flew to Whitehorse by airliner on Sept 26th, picked up a familiar

Bell 47 G3 turbo-charged helicopter, which was pretty much the same machine as I'd wrecked in the Bugaboos, and made the two-hour flight to Ross River.

The helicopter now sat next to at least a half dozen other helicopters scattered about just out of wind blast range of each other. Large numbers of red 45-gallon drums of fuel sat beside each helicopter. There were no corner gas stations so pilots hand-pumped every gallon into their machines. Ross River was in the midst of a staking rush with all the madness of the Klondike gold rush. But instead of mules laden with heavy packsacks struggling up the steep slopes, helicopters whisked the prospectors to and from their claims with ease. Al Kulan, who had rented my helicopter for the first few days to check up on his vast holdings, was a wealthy man, but you would never know it by his modest behaviour. He'd made a lot of the townspeople wealthy too. After two days flying together we became good friends and he invited me to his home for drinks and supper.

"Are we having cheese sandwiches?" I asked jokingly. Over a supper of moose steaks and a surprising assortment of vegetables and potatoes he told me the story of his prospecting years:

I started prospecting outa Ross River way back in 1954. After years of fruitless wandering over the Pelly Mountains, a large area of rusty rock caught my eye. I staked it with the help of my Dena friends and painstakingly searched every square inch of the area. All we had were rock hammers and determination. When we got short of supplies and tired of eating goat meat we all headed for Ross River heavily weighted down with rock samples. I was damn near broke so I took my best samples to Ben James, head geologist of Atlas metals, which was one of the local mining companies.

He poured over them for several days then called me in. 'Look Al,' he said, 'I've got a pack drill I can lend you. Why don't you take your boys back up there and drill a few holes. I'll stake you to a few weeks' grub.'

My Dena friends and I took turns carrying that bloody pack drill up to the claim. Another hard part was carrying cans of gas to run the damn thing. By the end of a week, we had more holes sticking in that rock than a porkypine has quills sticken' out. Trouble with the pack drill is you could only drill a very small diameter hole, and just a few feet down. Never drilled into anything exciting and the food ran out again. We returned to Ross River feeling just a little beaten up. Now I was really broke and had to quit for a while. I bummed around and did some prospecting for other companies.

In 1964, I managed to raise money by selling shares in a company that I had formed called Dynasty. I also staked a whole bunch of other properties before winter set in. I spent yet another winter living on wild meat and anything else I could find that was edible and cheap. In the summer of '65 I found some Americans with a bit of money. Their company was called Cyprus Mines, out of Los Angeles. We started drillin' on my old property with one of their decent-sized diamond drills. We were soon over budget and they were ready to quit. I picked the final spot to set up the diamond drill knowing that this was my last chance. This time we finally drilled into the ever-elusive ore body.

I had only missed it by only a few feet with that small pack drill. All of a sudden everyone was interested in drilling in there. I'd managed to find one of the richest lead-zinc ore bodies in the country, if not in

the world. So now here in little-known Ross River we have one of the
biggest staking rushes going on since the Klondike gold rush.

Al paused for a moment as if in deep thought. While he'd been talking I'd noticed that *The Songs of a Sourdough*, a book of poetry published in 1907 by Robert W. Service, was sitting on the table beside him.

"My father was a poet and I had an uncle who could recite Robert Service for hours," I said, pointing to the book.

"Every respectable Yukon prospector probably carries this book around even if it's only used as toilet paper," he replied with a distant smile on his face. "Take it with you and read it while you're here, instead of fightin' over cheese sandwiches."

I spent several long days flying prospectors and geologists up into the mountains surrounding Al Kulan's property. I read the amazingly colourful earthy poems at night in my room, and while I sat in the helicopter waiting for the prospectors to drive their stakes and break rock. Within a week just about every square inch of unclaimed land now had hundreds of 4 inch by 4 inch pointed white-painted stakes proclaiming the new part-time owners. The stakes would be driven into the ground, tied to trees, or held firm by a mound of rocks. Many of the claims would never be worked on. The money spent on these very expensive helicopter flights had been raised by promoters of small penny stock companies in stock exchanges all over the country. Claims close to Kulan's find would rake in millions of dollars for these scoundrels who didn't even know what a pick axe was.

On the eighth day the weather turned miserable. The geologist I was flying with finally called it off early and we returned to Ross River.

"We're all finished here," he said, "so you can head back to Whitehorse tomorrow."

It had been a long frustrating day of flying in rain, and patches of wet snow as we attempted to climb up steep slopes clogged with cloud.

"Heck with that," I replied. "I'm outta here right now!"

I had no intention of spending one more night in this place. Those famous Whitehorse bars and dance halls I'd heard so much about were beckoning me. I filled the fuel tanks to the brim and had my map spread out on a drum trying to figure the best way out of here when Al Kulan sauntered over. The weather was not suitable for the direct flight over the mountains that I'd taken when I flew here a little over a week ago.

"Heard you're leaving," he said pointing at a spot on the map. "That's the lowest pass through the Pelly Mountains. You'll end up on the Yukon River just north of Lake Laberge. You can follow the river all the way to Whitehorse." He came close with a smile on his face and added, "Don't forget to look for the 'marge of Lake Lebarge.' See how it's spelt Laberge with an 'E' on your map. Robert Service misnamed the lake so it would rhyme in his poem, *The Cremation of Sam Magee.*"

I had read the poem over and over and was excited at the prospect of actually seeing that spot.

Ross River and Lake Laberge were separated by the Pelly Mountains, which was the same nasty country I'd been flying in all week. The pass that Al had pointed out on the map was the only possible route through to the Yukon River. Ominous clouds hung low in the valley, but when I finally emerged from the narrow pass everything below was wide and flat and in no time I was following the Yukon River south.

The river would lead me straight to Whitehorse. The lake appeared ahead in the gloom. It was really nothing more than a widening of the Yukon River carved out by a glacier thousands of years ago. Today the lake was deserted, but I knew that thousands of men had travelled by sternwheelers, hand-hewn small boats and rafts through this lake on their way to Dawson City. A small desolate peninsula jutting into the lake appeared ahead. A few scrawny pines seemed imprisoned in the rough gravel and barren rock that ran right to the water. Alders shivered eerily in the increasing wind.

"Don't forget to look for the 'marge of Lake Lebarge'," had been Al's final words.

"Could this be the place?" I asked myself.

What had inspired Robert Service to write this famous poem? Had he seen this desolate spot through the window of a sternwheeler, on foot, or had he just imagined it like so many of his stories of the Klondike gold rush? The route ahead to Whitehorse looked black with heavy clouds. Rain and sleet suddenly beat on the bubble, threatening to break it. The helicopter was creeping along at 70 with 40 mile per hour headwinds. I would run out of fuel before I got to Whitehorse less than 50 miles up the Yukon River. I decided to return to Ross River. As I made a wide slow turn over the mystical spot I recalled the first verse out of Robert Services poem:

> There are strange things done in the midnight sun
> By the men who moil for gold;
> The Arctic trails have their secret tales
> That would make your blood run cold;
> The Northern Lights have seen queer sights,
> But the queerest they ever did see

Was that night on the marge of Lake Lebarge
I cremated Sam McGee.

The tailwind whisked me back to Ross River. Instead of dancing and living it up in Whitehorse's famous dancehalls, I joined the boys at the bar once again for beer and cheese sandwiches.

The weather cleared over night and I was able to fly directly to Whitehorse next day just before dark. Ken Miller, the base manager in Whitehorse, met me as I landed at the airport. His face lit up when I told him about having to turn back over the marge of Lake Lebarge. Many years my senior, he was tall, lean, with a hawkish nose and sky blue eyes. He briefed me on details of an unusual flight he had booked for me the next day.

"A few days ago an airline pilot flying at 25,000 feet spotted a crashed airplane as he flew over a high pass just west of the airport at Aishihik. A helicopter pilot flying in the area flew over and took a quick look. Said there was a dead body inside the airplane. It was too rough for him to land and check out more details. We think it's the Cessna 150 that's been missing since last April 28th. An Alaskan bush pilot by the name of Frank Herne was attempting to do a non-stop flight from Fairbanks, Alaska to Tallahassee, Florida. Search and Rescue spent two weeks and thousands of dollars searching for his airplane at the time. No luck at all until now. You'll be flying an RCMP officer up there tomorrow morning at eight. In the meantime, let me show you Whitehorse. It's quitting time."

Once settled in his favourite pub with two huge frosty mugs of beer, we talked. It turned out that he was also a Robert Service fan. He was one of those rare breed of pilots who loved poetry and was writing a book about the Yukon.

After a long swig on his beer he said, "You know the old saying that pilots can't write and writers can't fly is a commonly held belief in the aviation world. Can you imagine what airline passengers would think if the intercom crackled to life and the pilot said, 'This is your captain speaking. I've just written a sonnet and would like to read it to you.'

"If you were to ask 100 pilots around the world if they had heard of Robert Service at least half would give you a funny look and shake their heads. I doubt that would happen here in the Yukon though. He's like God to everyone up here. In 1904 he boated up from Vancouver to Skagway, and then got on board the narrow-gauge railway that connected from tidewater to Whitehorse. It was called the White Pass and Yukon Route Railway. He was almost penniless, but he had been promised a job as bank teller with the Canadian Bank of Commerce in one of the few buildings in Whitehorse. It was still mainly a city of tents. It was probably during that time that he saw Lake Laberge from the deck of a sternwheeler and was inspired to write *The Cremation of Sam McGee*. I don't think he knew when he stepped off that train that he would become one of the most read poets of the 20th century."

Ken was as good a tour guide as he was a pilot. He dragged me from one bar to the next and by the end of the evening I knew Whitehorse pretty well. The Whitehorse of 1966 was one of the liveliest, wackiest towns I'd ever seen. The streets were crawling with itinerant prospectors and the rugged tourists, who for some reason saw fit to go north for their holidays instead of south like I was inclined to do. Gaudily dressed women, who boldly plied their trade, barely stood out from the other townspeople who wore everything but ties. Every third building was a drinking establishment of some kind and most of them sported a dance floor crowded with happy dancers. Whitehorse got its name from the rapids just north of the city. Many of the charming old buildings had been built during Robert Service's time, when the town was rapidly changing from a jumble of tents to the city it is today. Whitehorse was the terminus for the sternwheelers that travelled the upper Yukon River and its tributaries between Dawson City and Whitehorse for more than 50 years. One of the more famous sternwheelers, the *S.S. Klondike*, was in the process of being moved from its place in the shipyards onto land to become a national historic site.

The next morning it was warm and sunny. Cpl. Bob Albertson of the RCMP climbed on board the helicopter looking and smelling like someone had poured a bottle of Yukon over-proof rum all over him.

"Bit hung over, are we?" I quipped after we introduced ourselves.

"No use ruining two days," he replied with a grin.

We took off and headed for Aishihik, a small community about an hour's flight northwest of Whitehorse.

"What do you think we'll find?" I asked, glancing at the dot on the map he'd given me showing the location we were headed for.

"Don't have a clue, but I guess we're going to find out pretty soon."

After flying over the military airfield at Aishihik, which was established during World War II as part of the Northwest Staging Route, the gentle rolling hills rose sharply into craggy mountains. It was a long, slow, steep climb, but we finally made it to the top and skimmed over the mile-high alpine meadows. Small patches of snow still survived in some of the deep north-facing crevasses, but they would soon be covered in snow once again as September edged toward October. Pure white Mountain Sheep scurried for cover. Suddenly the airplane appeared. It was laying upside down in a box canyon at the end of a long valley that stretched miles to the north. The white underbelly of the aircraft stood out in stark contrast to the vast moonlike area of large grey rocks left behind eons before by a receding glacier. I wasn't surprised that it had been spotted so easily by the airline pilot during this short summer break.

Six months ago, at least twenty feet of snow would have covered the ground here, and the all white underbelly of the airplane would have been almost invisible. The helicopter pilot who had identified the airplane was absolutely right.

It appeared to be too rough to land. I finally found a spot to land fifty yards away from the aircraft. The turbo-charged helicopter had plenty of power to deal with the high altitude, but getting the skids safely balanced on the rock piles took some doing!

"This is going to be one of those tough ones," Bob said quietly, as he rummaged inside his packsack for a body bag. Even from this distance we could see that the pilot in the wreckage was dead. The nose of the small two-passenger Cessna was a broken mass of crushed metal, but strangely the cabin and landing gear and tail section were intact. The undamaged sections of the aircraft appeared to be brand new. I quickly deduced that the pilot, heavy with fuel and without enough power to climb over the top, had tried to turn around, stalled, hit the deep snow with great force and flipped over.

"It's Frank Herne alright, checks out," Bob said, comparing his notes with the registration numbers on the side of the aircraft. It was a gruesome and sad sight to behold. His left arm clad in a bright yellow winter flying suit seemed to be reaching out of the half open cabin to greet us. His frozen dehydrated hand had a large gold ring on the wedding finger which Bob gently slipped it off and put it in an evidence bag. His seat belt was undone and it appeared that he was killed by a hard impact with the roof of the cabin. Next to the body was a fuel tank in place of the passenger seat. It had ruptured. If there had been any fuel in the tank it had long since evaporated. I was of the opinion that the aircraft probably would have blown up if it hadn't been cushioned by at least 10 feet of snow.

"If you don't mind taking a look around, I'll take care of the body," Bob said.

I was very happy to oblige him. While he undertook the grim task of getting the pilot into the body bag, I circled the airplane looking for anything that might help with the investigation.

Several hundred feet away I saw what looked like green leaves amongst the rocks, but there were no trees in this desolate place. As I moved closer, I couldn't believe my eyes. I was looking at American dollars scattered about all over the place. The first one I picked up was $20.00, the second $50.00. They were weather-beaten and some had been chewed by alpine rodents.

"There's money scattered all over the place," I shouted to Bob, who was tugging at the half-frozen body which seemed glued to the plane.

"Gather it up if you don't mind," he shouted in a strained voice.

Bob joined me in the search after completing the grim task of loading Frank Herne into the bodybag. We collected several hundred dollars worth of bills.

"We have to go," Bob finally said. "Let's count it together and I'll

The last remains of the Cessna 150.

seal it in an envelope. They told me he might have been carrying a lot of money on board."

Our job here was done. Investigators would come later. With the body strapped on the rack of the helicopter, we took off for Aishihik where an RCMP vehicle would be waiting. I couldn't help but think that this pilot who had dreamed of landing in Tallahassee to be greeted by throngs of cheering crowds, finally got to fly out of this valley. It just wasn't the way he intended. Bob directed me to land close to a dust and mud covered RCMP truck awaiting us at the airport. Bob and his assistant loaded Frank Herne's body into the truck. My job here wasn't finished. A man and a woman approached Bob and engaged in a heated conversation while I pumped some badly-needed fuel into the helicopter.

Finally, he pointed in my direction and they headed towards me avoiding the sparse shrubs that were growing out of the badly cracked tarmac. I'd been told that an American insurance investigator was waiting for me at the airport. He was to be flown to the crash site. What I didn't expect was a woman as well.

"Hi, I'm Frank Herne's wife," she said in such a cheerful manner that I was a little stunned. Her dead husband was in the truck that was now moving away towards Whitehorse. The insurance agent was the one who looked glum. A money issue, no doubt. I took off with the two of them stuffed in the cabin and once again I climbed up the steep cliffs, over the grassy tundra and struggled with another landing at the site.

"Oh," she said when she saw the brown stain surrounded by gray hair, on the cabin roof of the airplane, "that must have been where he hit his head."

I was speechless and shivered when she said this with about the same emotion one would have looking at a stain on the carpet. While the two of them examined the aircraft I walked the fifty yards to the helicopter, got my sandwiches and my thermos of tea, sat on a rock and started to eat more out of necessity then out of enjoyment. I sure hadn't felt like eating up to now. A fifty dollar bill sat in the rocks waving at me in the slight breeze just a few feet from where I was sitting. Then I saw another and another. I had found the mother lode. I picked them up and stuffed them in my packsack along with the half-eaten ham and cheese sandwich. My appetite was gone. I had found gold, green gold and it was all mine. Like so many others in the Yukon, gold fever grabbed me. But what would the wife and insurance adjuster think about me down on my hands and knees moving and poking under rocks?

"Ah ha!" I said to myself remembering the rock hammer that I always carried in the helicopter. I managed to get the hammer without breaking an ankle. The geologists that flew with me weren't the only ones looking for mineral deposits. It had become a hobby of mine and I had managed to impress quite a few of them with my finds. I started pounding rock with my right hand and picking up bills with my left. Mrs. Herne and the insurance agent both stopped what they were doing and stared over the 50-yard distance with very curious looks on their faces.

"Checking for gold, it's a hobby of mine!" I shouted with a big grin on my face holding up the hammer. That seemed to satisfy them and they went back to their investigation totally oblivious of me. I scrounged in the rocks for more of the bills. By the time they were ready to leave, my stuffed packsack was sitting on the helicopter seat.

"I'll tie it on the rack outside," I said as Mrs. Herne slid into the seat beside me.

"No need to," she replied. "I'll carry it on my lap."

It was a short 15-minute flight to Aishihik, but with Mrs. Herne sitting with my pack on her lap it seemed like the longest flight I'd ever made. Downdrafts had me struggling up the slopes in monotonous circles. Winds seemed to slow me to a sloth's pace. I finally landed at the airport beside a cache of red fuel drums and shut down. I would need more fuel for the trip home. The insurance agent climbed out, ducked instinctively to avoid the still turning rotors and left Mrs. Herne and me sitting tightly side by side. She slowly slid over into his seat and placed my pack on the seat between us I imagined her glaring at me and saying, "What's in the pack it's bigger than when we flew in?" Instead she said, "Did you find any gold?"

"Nope, nothing but bare rock," I replied, climbing nervously out of the helicopter. I hoped she didn't notice the sweat on my brow or the slight twitch in my eye. Maybe I should give her the money. No, it's mine, my scrambled brain said. Insurance will cover it, I rationalized.

"I'll wait for the rotors to come to a complete stop, they make me nervous," she said, placing her hand casually on my packsack. I didn't think the rotor blades would ever come to a stop, but they finally did and Mrs. Herne slowly climbed out and headed towards the insurance agent, who was standing off in the distance looking impatient and annoyed. I fuelled up in a hurry, got the heck out of there and headed gleefully for Whitehorse. Ken Miller was there once again to greet me.

"How'd it go?" he asked.

"I had a great day," I replied. "Drinks are on me tonight."

That elicited a strange look from him. He knew that I'd gone out to pick up a dead fellow pilot.

"Sorry, I have a date with my wife so you'll have to party alone. Take tomorrow off though. You've earned it."

I drove the old Ford company truck into town, bought a bottle of over-proof rum and headed up to my room in the old and famous Whitehorse Inn. I poured a couple of fingers of rum into a glass then changed it to a couple of thumbs and set the bottle beside the old black dial phone on the side table. I picked up my packsack and dumped the contents on the bed. They looked like dried leaves on a compost heap. Like old Scrooge, I patiently flattened the crinkled bills, placed them into piles of 10's, 20's, 50's and 100's and counted them. My god! I suddenly realized that I had at least half a year's wages here! I picked up a few of them and stuffed them in my pocket. I put the rest in an empty laundry bag which I hid in the corner under my bed. After another nip of rum I locked the hotel door and headed for the infamous bar downstairs.

It was a quiet night and a local band called The Canucks was playing to a few dancing couples. I was surprised to see an older man sitting at the almost deserted long and ornately carved turn of the century bar. He was wearing a Klondike Helicopters hat identical to the one I was wearing, except his looked brand new. Mine, in true helicopter pilot tradition was a filthy, sweat-stained hat that clung to my head 'til death do us part.

If I ever lost it which was unlikely, I would get a new one, throw it in a swamp, drag it out and beat it in the dirt before I'd ever be seen wearing it. I sat down beside the old man and ordered a drink.

"What the hell is that, looks counterfeit," the bartender said when I slammed down a faded, chewed-up American twenty on the counter. "Oh, sorry, wrong bill," I mumbled stuffing it back in my pocket totally embarrassed. I was scrounging around for a Canadian bill when the old man turned toward me.

"Put that money away. I'm buyin'. You know there was a time when you could come in here and buy a drink with one of these," he said plunking a handful of gold nuggets on the counter and sitting himself on the bar stool beside me. "Now ya gotta pay with this green stuff." He slid a large bill to the bartender and ordered a drink for himself as well. His deeply lined face was almost hidden by long scraggly grey hair, but his clothes looked neat and fresh. I stared at the beautifully shaped nuggets each one the size of a thumbnail.

"Name's Isaac Crew," he added, reaching out a knurled hand and giving me an almost toothless grin. "Been workin' a placer claim on a creek just north of here for years and finally hit pay dirt. See you got a Klondike hat on your head. Wadda you do?"

When I told him a look of amazement came over his face.

"Well I'll be darned," he said. "Your partner, Ken Miller, has flown me into my claim far too many times to count, always gave me a special deal. Seems like you hit pay dirt too from the looks of that bill you put on the table. Let's have a look."

The last thing I wanted to do was show off one of these bills, but I couldn't very well refuse a man who had just brought me a drink.

"Looks real enough to me," he said peering closely at the holes, "but a rat musta thought it was dinner. Where the heck did you find it?"

I knew that bloody question was coming.

"Found it in a trapper's cabin," I said breaking out in a sweat wondering how many more times I would have to tell this false tale. I brought Isaac a drink to even the score and after some forced small talk I left.

The next day it turned cold with a hint of snow in the air. I hung around the hotel feeling restless and out of sorts. Finally, at three I got tired of my endless pacing and picked up the copy of *The Songs of a Sourdough* that Al had given me. Four lines from one of Robert Service's poems kept haunting me.

> *I wanted the gold, and I sought it,*
> *I scrabbled and mucked like a slave.*
> *Was it famine or scurvy – I fought it;*
> *I hurled my youth into a grave.*

The bottle of rum still sat next to the telephone. I wanted desperately to pick up the bottle and take a sip or two of the delicious liquid. Instead, I picked up the phone and made a call.

Cpl. Albertson met me on the steps of the RCMP office.

"I found a few extra bills on my second trip up there," I said as I handed him a brown bag stuffed with the crumpled money

It was a long walk back to the hotel and I took it slow. The yellow setting sun snuck out of the ominous snow clouds painting the almost deserted streets gold with a touch of silver. My body felt lighter, livelier and there was a bit of my Irish grandfather's dance step to my walk.

CHAPTER SEVEN

THE MAD IRISHMAN

The mining camp was located on the north shore of Earn Lake, a beautiful lake 160 miles north-east of Whitehorse. I had relieved the helicopter pilot here a month ago, a few days after my trip to Aishihik with Cpl. Albertson. It was nice to be back flying a Hiller 12E again. Ernie Grant, my engineer friend in Fort Smith, was also here looking after the helicopter. We watched as the same Beaver aircraft and pilot that had flown me here from Whitehorse taxied into the dock just a few feet from where the helicopter was parked. On my trip in, I'd gotten to know the pilot, a veteran who'd survived 30 years of Yukon bush flying.

As the sole passenger staggered out of the Beaver, the last warm sun of the year caught his red hair, grey-speckled beard, and ruddy freckled face. The deep wrinkles on Paddy O'Reilly's face didn't hide the life in his eyes, or the roguish charm about him, but he looked old from hard work, booze and obviously a recent scrap. He had a black eye and bruises on his face to prove it.

I remembered what head driller Dick Murphy had told me earlier when he'd heard that Paddy was coming to work for him.

"The man's a legend! I should be workin' for him," he'd said. "Paddy could work 24 hours a day on these bloody drills and never blink an eye. About a dozen years ago when I was just a helper, we were drilling together up in the Arctic. There were polar bears everywhere and we were scared shitless of them. A polar bear will eat you just for somthin' to do.

"One night we were hangin' out in our tent freezing our nuts off when a claw the size of a skinning knife sliced through the tent and a huge polar bear stuck his head right in the tent near where Paddy lay. Paddy didn't hesitate for a second.

"He poked that polar bear right in the nose. Gave him a big nose bleed and sent him runnin'. Got in the papers an' all and Paddy became famous.

"If there's a brawl in a bar anywhere in the world Paddy's probably going to be in the thick of it," Dick added merrily.

Now his legendary hero stood there bleary-eyed and inebriated.

"You're drunk as a toad in a rotten turnip, ya old bugger," Dick Murphy said, "and now I gotta work your shift tonight while you sleep it off."

"It's been a right soft day, but that over-proof rum they serve in Whitehorse has hit me hard," Paddy mumbled.

"Crank the chopper up, Hank," Dick snorted at me. "I'll put this useless tit to bed and you can fly me back out to that greasy drill site again. I'll hafta work the night shift for him."

I sensed, actually smelled Ernie behind me. He'd acquired an authentic Inuit hand-made caribou parka on one of his northern trips and he wore it with great pride. It was designed for very cold days. Other times the musky odour was enough to turn stomachs inside out. It didn't bother Ernie one bit.

"Jeez," he said, "Dick's in a fit. Sure glad I'm not flyin' with ya."

"Me, too," I replied moving away from that parka.

That night while Paddy slept off the booze, the temperature plummeted. We all scurried to our tents and tried to keep warm. Ernie and I lived in a small two-man tent. Even though the rusty tin heater was red hot the inside of the tent wall was covered with ice.

It was not a great night for sleeping. We took turns stoking the almost useless fire.

Around midnight a loud noise woke me up. My first thought was that I'd never heard Ernie snore that loud. It wasn't him. His huge frame filled the open tent flap. He was staring intently at the lake. By now the noise had grown tremendously. I crawled out of my arctic sleeping bag and joined Ernie at the tent flap. The lake was moving. The thin crust of ice that had formed on the lake was expanding rapidly. Great slabs of slate-like ice were building up on the shore of the lake. To quote Robert Service, "It *cracked and growled, roared and howled,*" all night. I wondered if Paddy was sleeping through all this.

He was up early with the rest of us, a little flawed, but ready for work. After breakfast which he hardly touched, I flew him out to the drill. As I approached I saw Dick standing beside the helicopter pad, eyes looking like battleship guns.

"Hope you had a nice night, Paddy," he growled. "Now get your Irish arse to work while I go get some sleep."

Not a word came forth from Paddy. He ambled to the drill site, a stark steel tower surrounded by a rough plywood shack covered in ice and snow.

When I picked Paddy up towards dark, he'd done his job, but was a pretty tired looking fellow.

The next day things changed for the Irishman. He made it to breakfast, but he was looking much the worse for wear. Dick took one look at him and asked, "You going to make the day?"

"I'll be gettin' on with it for sure," Paddy replied testily.

I dropped Paddy and his assistant Pete at the drill site and headed back to camp with the exhausted night crew on board. Two men at a time, driller and helper work on a diamond drill site. The men barely have time for a pee break. One shift is from dawn to dusk, the other dusk to dawn. It's cold, filthy, back-breaking work. Their only reward is they're probably the highest paid men in the mining industry.

I'd barely shut the helicopter down when I saw Dick scampering towards me. This wasn't the calm, cool, competent driller who ran his crew smooth as grease. Now he looked mighty agitated.

"We're buggered, Hank," he blurted out when I climbed out of the helicopter. "I've gotta go out and replace the drunk again. His helper called on the radio, says Paddy's acting weird."

"OK," was my reply, taking special note of Dick's homicidal look.

Paddy wasn't giving him many moments of sleep. When a very cranky Dick and I arrived at the drill site, Pete the assistant was waiting for us.

"Paddy's acting crazy. He's wandered off into the bushes looking for someone called Jock."

The drill site where Dick and I went chasing after Paddy.

I shut down the chopper and the two of us followed Paddy's tracks in the snow.

Pete tended to the drill site. A huge propane burner, which heated water to lubricate the ever-demanding diamond drill, needed constant monitoring to avoid a total freeze-up.

We found Paddy sitting on a stump talking to someone. Whoever it was, I certainly didn't have enough Irish blood in me to see him. We coaxed Paddy back to the helicopter and I took off towards camp, leaving Dick to work yet another shift. The radio crackled to life.

"The camp's fogged in solid," the radio dispatcher said.

Sure enough the huge mass of freezing water that I'd left glistening in the early morning sun not long ago was now nothing but a big patch of fog. It blended like spilt ice cream with the snow-covered mountain that served as its northern backdrop. The first touch of sun would melt the frost and then ripples from the lake would join in a frenzy to form fog as dense as grandma's nightie. But all was usually forgiven towards noon when sun power drove the white gloom away.

All I had to do was wait. The fog wouldn't have bothered me a bit if it weren't for my passenger. I radioed back with a barefaced lie.

"No problem," I said. "We'll just hang out here in the sun."

I picked a small swamp, landed and shut down. Paddy sat quietly beside me until all the moving parts of the helicopter stopped.

Then the grunting started. Was I hearing things? It sounded like a bunch of flatulent tuba players warming up. I didn't know what to expect from Paddy on this flight, but I sure didn't expect these sounds.

It took me a while to figure out the grunts weren't coming from Paddy. It was moose rutting season and there was a full symphony orchestra of them performing out there.

Paddy started imitating them and the old fool did it just a little too well. All of a sudden a huge bull moose came hammering through the trees, shaking his head and knocking down the brush like a lawn mower. Steam poured out of his nostrils, making him look like a charging locomotive. *If this enormous beast thinks that the helicopter looks like another bull, he just might charge us.*

I did the safest and most sensible thing I could do under the circumstances. I left poor Paddy sitting in the helicopter and climbed up on the mast. Then I fired three shots in the air from my .357 magnum pistol trying to scare the big bull moose off.

Two things happened almost in an instant. Paddy jumped out of the

The bull moose that charged Paddy and I, as he makes his retreat.

helicopter and started running around the edge of the swamp shouting, "Jock, Jock, they're shooting at me!"

And, after shaking his huge head and rattling his horns against the bushes, the big bull moose made a hasty retreat. I don't think it had anything to do with the gun fire. The Irishman had scared the hell out of him.

When the fog finally burned off at Earn Lake, I coaxed Paddy back into the helicopter and flew him to camp.

Paddy stayed in camp the next day as well. Everyone hoped that a little rest might put him back together. When we sat down for supper Paddy looked much better.

He even talked to Dick about the good old days. You could see the relief on everyone's faces, especially Dick's.

At supper time we all dug into big slabs of roast beef and platters of potatoes and vegetables. It was a happy crew until Paddy started putting bits of meat on his shoulder. All idle chatter ceased.

Pete said, "What the bloody hell are you doing, Paddy?"

"I'm feeding the leprechauns," he replied casually.

I think I did see a little green man sitting on Paddy O'Reilly's shoulder eating bits of meat. "Blimey!" I said to myself. Was I seeing things after what had happened today or were the genes I'd inherited from my Irish grandfather making me bonkers?

In any case, I casually put a bit of meat on my own shoulder. The silence in the cook tent was deafening. The men stared at me and their eyes said, "Oh no, now we have two crazies and Hank is our only way of this frozen shit-hole right now."

Dick saved me! He calmly reached up and put a piece of steak on his shoulder. One by one, the rest of the men followed suit and we ate in silence.

Things went from bad to worse. At night Paddy would wander around the camp screaming, "The leprechauns are going to kill me!"

Or, he'd simply wander off into the woods shouting, "Jock, where are you?"

And the final straw was when he grabbed an axe and scurried around the camp chasing the imagined little men. His weird behaviour had us all scared to death.

At night we lay freezing in the dark, wondering if we were going to be mercilessly put to death. We lived in tents. How do you lock a canvas door?

Landing at the camp at Earn Lake.

And as Ernie said, "How do I know he doesn't think I'm a freakin' leprechaun?"

"We gotta get Paddy outa here. I've known the old bugger for years and I never saw him behave like this," Dick declared.

We tried the next morning, when he seemed a little more sane than usual. We'd been through hell in the frozen Yukon and all of us were ready to join Paddy in some asylum if we couldn't get him out of this camp.

The Hiller 12E is just about the only two-passenger chopper where the pilot sits in the middle. Dick coaxed Paddy into the left seat and buckled him in so tight the poor man could hardly breathe. Then he came around and sat in the right seat. He was riding shotgun.

The whole crew plus one husky pup that belonged to one of the drillers stood around watching.

"At last we're rid of him!" every face proclaimed. I was not happy about being stuck in the middle next to this nut case, but Paddy was behaving almost normal.

The nearest road was at Pelly Crossing 60 miles west where we'd arranged a truck to pick this madman up. I started the helicopter and took off. Everything went fine for the first minute.

Then Paddy screamed, "The leprechauns are gonna wreck the helicopter!"

He grabbed my hand and pushed down hard. As always my left hand was on the collective which controls the pitch on the rotors. The helicopter went straight down 200 feet and in an instant was almost into the trees.

I used every bit of strength I had to pull the collective back up against him. At last he let go and grabbed the door screaming, "Lord Jesus, here I come!"

He climbed out the door onto the skid. We were over trees. The only place to land was back at camp. I poured the power on and headed for the pad.

Paddy seemed frozen to the skid. I made the worst and hardest landing on the pad that the poor helicopter would ever make. I knew Ernie would say, "Now you've really buggered my baby."

The look on everyone's face said, "Why didn't he do us a favour and jump?"

I kind of felt the same. Paddy just stood there on the skid as if nothing had happened.

"Let's tie the fool up," someone suggested.

"Let's throw him in the lake," someone else said half seriously.

Ernie, the fixer, settled the whole issue. "I'll keep an eye on the poor bugger," he said.

Each time Paddy ran off into the woods looking for Jock, Ernie followed his tracks and brought him back. He hovered over the man every second, sometimes well into the night. The helicopter was not quite as spotless as usual, but drill grease and dirt was preferable to having Paddy on the loose.

Paddy finally got over the DTs or whatever it was that had made him delirious, and the ice on the lake finally froze enough that it would hold an airplane. One was sent from Whitehorse equipped with skis. The big question for bush pilots in the fall is when to switch from summer floats to winter skis. Airplanes with floats attached don't land well on ice and snow. Airplanes on skis can't land on water at all.

The problem was the ice had suddenly settled, leaving at least 3 inches of water on top which in my opinion didn't make for a very safe landing. Fortunately, this was once again the same Beaver aircraft and pilot who'd flown Paddy and me in here previously. The water didn't seem to bother him at all. He circled several times and then came in to land. We all stood here holding our breath as the plane descended lower and lower and finally hit the water.

Freezing water exploded over the aircrafts hot engine forming a ghostly contrail. Waves spread from the thin layer of water like a tsunami. The ice held and the aircraft taxied to the rickety dock.

On board was more food, supplies and an unexpected replacement pilot for me.

"That was the hairiest landing I've ever made," the pilot said to me as we unloaded the airplane.

"Well let me tell you," I replied, "I'm impressed."

We loaded Paddy and his scruffy bags aboard the airplane. I'm sure Paddy could have finished out a shift or two, maybe even worked forever, but no one in camp was of a mind to keep him around. I followed with my quickly assembled effects. Mail, core samples and a few odds and ends were the only other things to accompany us. I'll never forget that takeoff. The plane seemed glued to the water forever. After all I'd been through I didn't want to end up at the bottom this lake well preserved until spring. Finally the roar of gushing icy water subsided and we were safely airborne on course for Whitehorse.

Paddy and I sat in awkward silence well into the flight which suited me fine. No one had gone through the personal hell he'd put us through more than Ernie and me.

Then Paddy suddenly blurted out, "I'm sorry it's gone badly between us."

"That's OK," I replied not really meaning it. Then it occurred to me that Earn Lake was behind us both now even though I knew we were going in different directions.

I was going home for a much needed rest. The president of my company would say to me, "Well done, Hank, great job." Then I'd collect my Christmas bonus. As for Paddy, I highly doubted this man would ever work as a diamond driller again. I looked at him sitting there. His eyes no longer sparkled, his red hair and grey-speckled beard were stained and filthy and his once ruddy face deathly pale.

"Used to be married and have a son and daughter, but ain't seen them in years," Paddy said, interrupting my thoughts.

"You know this life sure isn't for families," I finally replied, thinking about my own disintegrated marriage. Once again we lapsed into silence and I stared out the small windows at the Yukon Mountains glistening with fresh snow.

"I play a fiddle, you know," he said quiet enough that I barely heard it over the drone of the Beaver's engine.

Memories flooded over me. My long dead Irish grandfather had been a lovable rogue who had played a fiddle and sang wonderful Irish ballads. He also kept bottles of rum stashed all over the house.

"Do you know this one?" I asked and stumbled through one of my grandfather's songs that had been rooted in my brain since I was eight. He always sang it with tears in his eyes.

"There'll be no one to welcome you home [No, my boy]
No one to welcome you home,
For when you return to the land of your birth,
There'll be no one to welcome you home."

Halfway through the song I was delighted to hear Paddy singing along with me.

"I do know that one, son," he said, his eyes lighting up for the first time in days. "Did you know that song is about a young man who left Ireland for Canada. When he finally returned to Ireland years later his family were all dead. He was a fiddler himself and wrote music to the poem which he found in his mother's belongings."

After landing at the airport in Whitehorse we shared a cab to town.

Paddy got out, threw his meagre belongings over his shoulder and took a few steps towards his favourite bar. Then he turned, and walked back.

"Would ya be wantin' to be sharing a beer with me, lad?" he asked.

I mulled this over. I liked this crazy Irishman and I sure wanted a beer after months in a dry camp.

"Alright," I finally said.

I got my things out of the taxi and in no time we were through the door and into what looked more like a dance hall. The place was livelier than an Irish wake. I knew that Paddy, the legend, had found his stomping ground.

One man shouted, "There's the man."

A few others waved at him, but the majority gave him a furtive look and returned to what they were doing. This was a driller's hangout for sure. Unshaved men with oil-stained clothes danced with gaudy lipsticked girls.

We weaved and dodged through frolicking dancers and finally bellied up to the bar. I ordered two large mugs of beer. The bartender arrived with one, and shoved it in front of me.

"I can serve you a beer, but not this man," he said.

There was as sudden hush in the room as Paddy jumped up, pushed me aside and put his face so close to the bartender they almost touched noses.

"I'll be wantin' to know what you mean by what you just said," he growled.

I imagined I saw him with an axe in his hand again. But the glare in his eyes showed more anger than insanity.

"Paddy, me boy, we've had enough of your shenanigans. You were knackered when you left my place last time leaving a lot of broken glass, bruises and blood. No more, my friend. You want to go back to your hell-hole, do it somewhere else."

"That'll be what I'll be doing, you Irish arse. Just leave me be."

Then Paddy's eyes softened as he turned to me. "Sorry for this mess I've got you in. You're a good man, my friend."

With that said, Paddy headed for the door, bent over and weary looking. People gave him a wide berth. He gave one sad last look at everyone and left.

The din in the pub soon returned to normal. I sat and quietly drank my beer; then ordered another and another. I was ignored by the men and women sitting close to me.

"Is there a pay phone here?" I asked the bartender.

He pointed without saying a word. I picked up the phone, inserted a bunch of coins *clunk* by *clunk* and dialled my home phone in Calgary hoping that one of my children would answer.

CHAPTER EIGHT

DEAD RECKONING

The early morning flight from Vancouver to Prince Rupert was quite pleasant until we made our final approach to the airport. The old DC-6 shook violently in the wind whipped turbulence. Most of my fellow passengers were clinging to their armrests with white knuckles and whiter faces. But in spite of this, the pilot landed smoothly onto the runway. We taxied towards the small terminal, but parked a good distance away. The rain pelted down on us as we all waded our way across the tarmac to the terminal.

"They won't be flying to Stewart in this weather," I said to myself as I headed for the phone to reserve a hotel room in Prince Rupert.

The loudspeaker crackled and came to life. "The flight to Stewart will be leaving in 15 minutes," the voice announced.

Seven of us lined up at the Trans Provincial ticket counter, got our passes and tried to check our baggage.

"Oh no," the dumpy ticket agent said. "You have to carry your own bags to the aircraft."

We all trundled to a yellow airplane sitting a great distance from the terminal. I recognized it as a Grumman Goose twin engine amphibious aircraft. It was built in 1937, the same year I was born and would probably still be around when I die of old age. A man stood on top of the aircraft's nose where open hatches waited for our luggage. He was oblivious to the rain soaking his tattered blue jeans and leather jacket.

"Hi, I'm Captain Tom Miller, your pilot," he shouted over the rain pelting against the wings. "Now if you just pass me up your bags, we'll get loaded and take off to Stewart in no time."

I pushed my rain-soaked suitcases up to Tom and helped lift some of the other luggage up as well.

Tom slammed the hatches shut and slid smoothly down the side of the aircraft onto the tarmac. He was handsome, fit looking man, but his eyes had the raggedy look of a pilot with too many tough miles under his belt. He ushered the prettiest of the women into the cockpit beside him and left the rest of us to fend for ourselves. We all clambered aboard, climbing over boxes of freight and found a seat. I managed to get a front seat with a view into the cabin.

"This is my first trip to Stewart," I said as Tom started the port engine which sent out a belch of acrid smoke. "Is the weather always this bad?"

"Hell, this is nothing. We fly in this stuff all the time," Captain Tom replied with a grin on his face as he started the starboard engine. I'm sure his soothing tone of voice was the same one used by the captain of the *Titanic* before the ship hit the iceberg. We took off into the rough wet gloom. The clouds were barely clear of the tree tops. After ten minutes of being bounced around like a gull flying in a hurricane, the trees finally give way to rocky beaches and we were flying low over the choppy waters of a wide inlet. The turbulence was much lighter.

I thought that I would have been much happier in a helicopter. The steep cliffs on both sides of us came closer and closer together as we entered what I was to later learn was the more narrow Portland Canal, a 71-mile-long fiord misnamed by Captain Vancouver centuries before. A snowstorm hit us without warning. The mountains on both sides of us disappeared in the dense whiteness. Wet and clingy snow began building up on the windscreen and wings. Tom put the aircraft in a screeching nose dive, levelled off at the last second and landed in the choppy water. It sounded more like we were landing on a rock pile. Water vaporized into steam as it splashed over from the engines and momentarily blinded our view, but as we came to a floating stop I noticed that the salty water had cleaned the snow completely off the airplane.

Tom cut off the engines, turned to us and said in his patronizing voice, "Now don't you folks worry one little bit, these snow storms only last a few minutes. We'll be off for Stewart in no time."

Most of the passengers grudgingly accepted this as the situation. Minutes passed in almost total silence. Since we had nothing else to do I thought we should do a little chatting. It's always been my area of expertise, as Ernie always told me.

"This is my first trip to Stewart," I said to everyone. "I'm relieving Bud Tipping, the helicopter pilot, up there for two months. Do any of you know him?"

Tom was the first to answer, which surprised me considering the fact he was in the cockpit deeply engrossed in conversation with Suzy Cooper, who seemed quite comfortable sitting in the co-pilot's seat.

She'd been giggling constantly at whatever he said. I'd overheard her saying she was waitressing at the King Eddie, wherever that was.

"You can have that job," he shouted to me. "Flyin' over glaciers in the winter isn't somthin' I want to be doing. At least I have water under my backside."

I thought that was a strange thing for him to say considering the fact that he was the reason we were all sitting here instead of a nice comfortable hotel in Prince Rupert. A pleasant-faced woman sitting behind me was the next person to answer my question.

"Everybody knows everybody in Stewart," Mrs. Hadley said. "I've lived in Stewart for 20 years and I've seen lots of ups and downs. Right now it's roaring, what with Granduc building a mine site and whole subdivisions in town."

"Glad to meet you, son. Thanks with the help with the suitcases," barked Jim Waterford, reaching out a hand. He was wrinkled and old as the hills, but the twinkle in his eyes made him look young as talkative Suzy. "I'm the town clerk and just back from Victoria where I had to do some arm bending to get a few more dollars for snow removal. This is a bad year for snow."

I was destined to become close friends with Jim Waterford and Mrs. Hadley in years to come. They both told me that this wasn't the first time they'd been sitting in a snowstorm in the middle of this canal.

"Jim and I have learned to pack lunches for this trip," Mrs. Hadley said.

Two rough-looking men sitting near the back told me they were miners working for Granduc Mines, the company I would be contracted to. That was the limit of their conversation as they immersed themselves in girly magazines.

A thin, attractive freckle-faced young woman was sitting across from me. Up to this point she'd been very quiet, but she seemed as worried about our situation as I was. Now looking at me with roguish eyes she said, "So you're a helicopter pilot. Bet you wish you were in one now. This weather is so skungy."

"Sounds like you can read my thoughts," I replied, thinking that 'skungy' must be Australian for awful because her crisp accent told me that she was from *down under*.

"This is not only my first trip to Stewart, but it's the first time I've ever seen snow. I'm here as an exchange teacher until the end of the school year. My name's Jan Wilder," she said, reaching out her hand.

I took it and introduced myself. From there on we talked like we'd known one another forever. I was so mesmerized by her forthright personality that an hour passed by like it was minutes.

I didn't even notice that a big patch of blue had formed above us and the sun was shining through it. It was close to noon and both Jim and Mrs. Hadley were eating. Tom interrupted our reverie.

"Sorry, folks, just got a radio call from Stewart. They're snowed in. We're going to return to Rupert. Now didn't I tell you the storm would pass? It'll be smooth sailing from here on. Just look at that fine weather."

His voice reminded me of a cooing dove. Everyone groaned. We took off and headed back the way we'd come. It seemed like a good decision until the sun and blue sky changed into angry low clouds.

"Hank, could you come give me a hand?" Tom shouted back from the cockpit. The young lady sitting in the co-pilot's seat was happy to relinquish her place and I became a co-pilot in an airplane that I'd never even been in before. The last thing I saw was Jan's anxious face as Tom closed the cabin door. I have no doubt that the rest of the passengers were also a little worried. I couldn't believe what Tom did then.

"I don't actually need your help, but I sure do hafta pee badly," he said grinning at me. He dragged a container from under the seat, all the while somehow managing to hold the plane steady. After the can was safely stowed back under the seat he handed me an oil-stained wrinkled old map and a broken pencil.

"Just thought you might want to see the lay of the land," he added.

"Where are we?" I asked after patiently waiting for him to zip up. He pointed on the map. I peered out of the cockpit windows. A steep bluff on the left and an inlet on the right that ended at the mouth of a river made it easy to confirm our position. I noted the time from pure habit. The clouds and the ocean started coming together like a closing coffin. More snow hit us.

The waves below us were rapidly changing from choppy seas boiling whitecaps. The comfortable landscape of mountains and trees was fading away, being replaced by a white nothingness. Then the wind hit us viciously and fast, right on our tail.

Tom saw my look of dismay and said too nonchalantly, "We're in outflow winds blowing from out of the Nass Valley. Nothin' to worry about though. The tail wind'll get us into Rupert in no time."

My god, I thought, *I'm sitting next to an idiot*. Fog rolled in around us. I knew if we tried to land on the water the Alaskan King Crabs would be eating us and if we tried to turn we would probably be splattered all over one of those rock faces that loomed dark and close.

Our only option was to fly straight ahead. The weather just kept getting worse. When the only things we could see were the white caps, I knew we were in serious trouble.

All I could think about was the fact that I'd survived eight years as a jet pilot and two years flying helicopters, and was now going to die as a passenger in a Goose.

"Maybe you can figure out where we are," Tom mumbled, "I can't take my eyes off the waves."

Little did I realize when I'd casually marked our time and position on the map that I'd been, "dead reckoning" our position from shear habit as soon as I'd been given the map.

I remembered my old Air Force instructor saying, "*Dead Reckoning* is the process of estimating your position by advancing a known position using course, speed, time and distance. Christopher Columbus used DR to find America way back in 1492."

No longer was I thinking about dying. Now I was thinking about staying alive.

I'd been monitoring both the airspeed and magnetic heading since our last known location so I had all the information I needed to plot our position. I quickly drew our course on the map hoping the lead in the pencil didn't break. Then I put in hatch marks to measure our ground speed, taking into account our airspeed and the tail wind. The course I'd drawn on the map showed that we were heading right into a cliff. We would all be dead if I didn't make the right decision.

"Turn right 20 degrees," I ordered. Tom hesitated, glanced quickly at me with a look of doubt in his eyes, then made the turn slowly so as not to put a wing into the water.

A black shadow loomed up on our left then faded behind us. I continued plotting our course for the next terrifying twenty minutes. We finally flew clear of the raging sea into calm waters. Tom was not inclined to trust my primitive form of navigating forever and landed forthwith into the sea. The fog was so thick we could hardly see the wing tips. He cut the engines and we could hear waves crashing on rocks. Tom looked at me with fear in his eyes. Gone was the haughty grin.

"Thank you, my friend," he said. "Do you think we can keep this between ourselves?"

"Sure," I replied, "and just between us, I think we're about a half mile west of Port Simpson."

It didn't take us long to regain our composure. Then, Tom finally opened the hatch and told the passengers once again that there would be a bit of a delay. He had his bizarre sense of humour back.

"The important thing to remember is we aren't lost, just temporarily unsure of our position," Tom said.

I was glad to see the big grin back on his face. The passengers simply didn't understand this old pilot joke and just stared.

The chorus of questions and complaints from the very unhappy passengers all had to do with the fact that we'd once again landed in the middle of nowhere. Nobody realized how close to death they had all come, except Jan. She told me later that she could see it in my eyes.

"Gotta start up and go in circles so we don't hit those rocks," Capt. Tom announced to no one in particular, and that's exactly what we did for a very long time. Finally, the fog lifted just enough so we could see the shore. Sure enough there was the small village of Port Simpson off in the distance. We taxied in, docked and lined up at the nearest toilet.

I was soon to learn that this native village community also called *Lax Kw'alaams* or "place of the wild roses," was made up of nine different tribes. The villagers were wonderful. They fed us a meal that included smoked salmon and other local delicacies then showed us the local sights. As luck would have it a ship called the *Northland Prince* was scheduled to arrive around midnight to drop off supplies. It was virtually the lifeblood of this small village, which had no roads in or out. She made a trip up the west coast once a week from Vancouver. Stewart was its northernmost port and it was scheduled to arrive there first thing Saturday morning with passengers and tons of freight. Tom arranged for the three women and me to sail on the boat at the expense of the airline.

"It may not be as much fun as flyin', but at least you'll be in Stewart by morning," he said looking directly at me.

The weather improved enough towards evening that Tom had just enough daylight to fly to Prince Rupert. The remaining passengers were going to spend the night in a hotel there. Jan and I spent the rest of the day getting to know each other better. We walked the almost untouched beaches, holding hands, sitting on wet logs and talking.

When darkness fell all of us were invited to the chief's house where bottles appeared out of nowhere. Mrs. Hadley didn't drink, but the rest of us sure did. Suzy got a little drunk, Jan and I just got tiddley. By the time midnight arrived we were all close friends.

The four of us scrambled aboard the *Northland Prince*. There were only two empty staterooms available.

"I'll take care of Suzy. She's probably going to get seasick," Mrs.

Hadley said with a laugh as she supported the wobbly young girl. Jan and I had to share the other one. When we entered our lodgings for the night we both laughed with relief. The stateroom had double bunks.

We talked well into the night.

"Oh, it's beautiful," Jan, exclaimed next morning as Stewart appeared out of the gloom surrounded by towering glacier-covered mountains. Fog mingled with chunks of ice that floated in the ocean around us. Alaska was on our left and Canada on our right. We stood close together shivering on the deck. It was the 22nd day of January, 1967.

The *Northland Prince* was docked and held firmly in place when Jan and I walked down the ramp holding hands like a couple of school children. Bud Tipping, the base helicopter pilot, was there to meet me. He was easy to spot because he was wearing a company hat and was leaning against the company truck. Lawrence Felt, the principal of the school, was there to meet Jan and was just as easy to recognize. He was the only one on the whole dock with a suit and tie. They both looked at us a little confused. Phone calls had been sent to them advising that we were arriving on the same boat. It was our bold display of affection for one another that baffled them. What the heck. Jan and I didn't understand it either. Introductions were short and a little awkward.

"See you later," we both mumbled as we were whisked away to our separate jobs.

Bud deposited my bags in the King Edward hotel, better known as the "King Eddie," then we headed for the airport which was just one long block away. There sat a Hiller SL4 helicopter. This was the only one that Klondike Helicopters owned and ever would own. The pilot sat in a single seat up front, with 3 seats for passengers behind him. It was like

Stewart and Portland Canal. The line running up Mt. Dolly is
the Canada-USA border. Hyder is on the lower left.

Flying the Hiller SL4 in Stewart.

a big, oversized Hiller 12E, but it had a powerful engine and was nicer to fly. It was a great helicopter except for one weird quirk. There was a 13-pound weight strapped in the cabin beside the pilot's seat.

"There's a centre of gravity problem with this machine. When you have 3 passengers in the cabin you attach this weight to a mount on the tail boom," Bud said, "and when you fly empty you have to mount it in the cabin."

He led me back to a mounting bracket inches from the tail rotor. I couldn't believe my eyes. How could any manufacturer design something so ridiculous? This would entail shutting down the helicopter ever time passengers were picked up or dropped off and waiting for the tail rotor to stop to avoid getting chopped up. I did this for two days then left the weight sitting in the cabin. Bud was a big man who weighed at least 30 lbs. more than me. In my mind, that solved the centre of gravity problem. Bud spent two hours teaching me how to fly the machine and briefing me on what I was supposed to do with it in this god-forsaken country. Then he jumped into the waiting Goose aircraft and headed for Rupert before the next snowstorm hit.

Granduc Mines, the company I was contracted to, was busy building a huge tunnel from its base camp called Tide Lake about 32 miles north of Stewart to a big copper ore body, 11 miles southwest into the Leduc Valley. They were tunnelling from both ends and hoped to meet somewhere in the middle. My job was to transport people and equipment to and from Stewart, Tide Lake and the huge camp at Leduc. This was the toughest country I'd ever flown in.

It never seemed to stop snowing and the winds above the tunnel blew constantly against huge craggy mountains filled with fog-shrouded glaciers that blocked every route. Each day, I would arrive back in Stewart haggard and worn out, but the town would always cheer me up. Jan and I were together pretty much every day. We visited Mrs. Hadley often in her big old house. She was a grandmother.

"I want nine of these," Jan said one day smiling up at me. She sat on the floor surrounded by Mrs. Hadley's laughing grandchildren.

"Finally got some money out of those tight-fisted son-of-a-guns down in Victoria," old Jim Waterford told me one day as we sat drinking a beer in the King Eddie.

When Bud finally returned from his holiday down south, I was ordered back to the head office in Calgary.

I was in love with this wonderful little town and the girl I'd met there. Jan's teaching contract ended in June and I was looking forward to meeting her in Vancouver in July.

CHAPTER NINE

THE BELL JET RANGER

When I arrived in Calgary from Stewart, I was overdue for some time off. It had been a long year of flying and I didn't even want to look at a helicopter.

After a week of loafing about and visiting with my kids, curiosity got the better of me and I dropped into Klondike's hanger to visit with fellow pilots and engineers. I hadn't seen Ernie for quite some time. He wasn't into bold displays of affection, but the bear hug he gave me nearly knocked me over and his greasy coveralls did permanent damage to my white tee shirt.

"Get yer lazy arse into Jim Lipinski's office," he said. "He's been trying to get hold of you."

I headed straight to Jim's office wondering what I'd done wrong this time.

"You know we ordered a Jet Ranger," Jim said, staring at my grease covered shirt, "which is due off the assembly line at Bell Helicopters in Fort Worth, Texas, on May 5th. We want you to go pick it up."

"You want me to go get it!" I'd replied completely dumbfounded. Every helicopter pilot in the company wanted to make that trip. "Why me?" I asked.

"Because you've earned it," he replied. "Now, let's go get a beer to celebrate." It seemed hard to believe that just a year ago I'd sat in this same office begging for a job.

I arrived in Dallas, a sister city to Fort Worth, on May 5th on Southwest Airlines. The company had a car waiting to transport me to the huge Bell Helicopter plant in Fort Worth, even though I was very small potatoes to them. They were far more involved in building military helicopters for Vietnam.

The city of Fort Worth, which spans over four counties, was a very strange community that seemed to have forgotten that prohibition was over. It was dry as stale popcorn. You couldn't buy a beer anywhere, but it hadn't forgotten the civil war. The local drugstore sold pistols and other gunnery like it was aspirin. All the hotels had bars which were called private clubs. If you wanted to drink there you had to be registered in a room, at which time you were issued with a very official membership card. I made good use of that card that night and turned up at Bell Helicopters vast factory at 8 AM next morning for a week-long ground school course.

"The 206A Bell Jet Ranger you're about to spend a lot of money on was once a loser, but I think you're going to love this helicopter anyway," the classroom instructor said with a slight smile on his face. The distant sounds of helicopters landing and taking off mingled with the constant chatter of rivet guns on the factory assembly line close by. The instructor's opening remark definitely got our attention.

"You can thank the US Army for the existence of the Jet Ranger," he added. "In 1962 the army decided they needed a lightweight, jet-turbine-powered, 4-passenger helicopter, so they created a financially lucrative competition for a light observation helicopter. Bell entered the competition and lost out to the Hughes OH-6 built by Hughes Helicopters, a company formed by the eccentric millionaire Howard Hughes way back in 1947. The military version of our helicopter was called a YOH-4. With a name like that how could we have possibly won? Since then we've done a lot of modifications to make it more commercially viable."

The instructor turned on a slide projector displaying all the specifications of this new helicopter.

"It's powered by an Allison 250-C18 A turboshaft jet engine that will give you a lot of power. Her top speed is 150 mph, roughly double the speed of those Bell 47s you've been flying. She can climb to 20,000 feet and has a range of 430 miles.

"She only weighs 1609 pounds empty with a maximum takeoff weight of 3,200 lbs., which would give you a payload of almost 1600 lbs. if you didn't need fuel. Speaking of fuel, this helicopter runs on Jet B which is a mixture of about 70% kerosene and 30% gasoline. The big airliners burn pure kerosene called Jet A, which produces static electricity as it passes through a refuelling hose, but it's not very explosive. Gasoline, however, is very explosive, but not static producing. Put the two together and you have a very unstable mixture running through a pump hose. Don't even think about fuelling up without a ground cable. We've just received a report of a Jet Ranger blowing up in Alaska. The engineer was refuelling from drums without using a ground cable. As he pulled the nozzle away from the tank, a static spark blew the tank to bits. Fortunately, the blast was so powerful that it blew itself out with no fire. All three men standing beside the helicopter were covered in fuel, but luckily the only thing hurt was their pride. The concussion caused them to mess their pants. The Jet Ranger has a grounding jack right next to the fuel cap. Use it!"

As the instructor rattled on in his engaging humorous tone, I glanced around. Of the three of us who sat in the classroom, I was the only Canadian. Stan Morris, an instructor from Van Nuys, California had scraped every penny together to buy a Jet Ranger for his small company. Louis Rizzo, the other student, was a rich sombre-looking Italian who'd arrived here with a beautiful blonde girl half his age.

"I buy des helicopter to fly around Europe with my little blonde mink," he'd said the night before when we all met at the hotel private club. The pretty blonde had spent the whole evening stroking his hair and doting over him. This morning Louis was already nodding off beside me and the ground school course had barely started. I suspected he'd been up late.

A little more than a month before I'd been fighting snow and ice in Stewart and certainly didn't expect to be sitting in an air conditioned classroom in Fort Worth Texas where the outside air temperature was well over 100 degrees.

By May 10th, I was finished with the ground course and commenced flying training. My first surprise was to find out that the pilot flew from the right seat instead of the left as was standard on all the Bell 47 models. My instructor's name was Jim Bell.

"Don't own the company," he said, "but I'm sure my last name helped me get this job."

The second surprise was to find out that, unlike Bell 47s, there was no clutch. The Allison engine slowly wound up as smooth as velvet. The tail rotor and a thousand moving parts came to life in short seconds. Once the throttle was opened to full power everything was automatic. It was a simple matter of raising and lowering the collective and gently manipulating the very sensitive cyclic. Autorotations were feather-like. There was a gentler rate of descent, and the long heavy rotors had lots of inertia built into them, making for a very comfortable landing. This helicopter was nothing like anything I'd ever imagined. Comparing the Bell 47 to a Jet Ranger was like going from a Model T Ford to a luxury Cadillac. The spacious rear cabin seated three. The pilot and one passenger sat in the front. Instead of cargo racks there was a huge cargo hold behind the cabin. After five days, I was totally checked out on the helicopter and ready to head for Calgary.

"Y'all come back now," Jack Bell said to me in his soft Texan voice as I started the helicopter to head for home.

Four days later I landed in Calgary. This was only the fourth Jet Ranger to enter Canada. It took three days do all the custom and import paperwork. Then I had the privilege of taking Jim out for his first check ride.

"How does it feel being the instructor for a change?" he said with a huge grin on his face.

"Great!" was my simple reply.

My plans to meet Jan in Vancouver in July didn't happen. The new

Refueling the Jet Ranger at the seismic
camp. A shot of the portable driller.

jet helicopter was scheduled to go on a six-month contract with an oil
exploration company called Ray Geophysical in Northern Alberta. I was
destined to be there for most of it.

The trailer camp we stayed in there was situated near a small airstrip
in the middle of muskeg and swamp. The mosquitoes tortured us in July.
The blowflies and mosquitoes tormented us in August. Wasps joined the
fleet in September.

My primary flying job was to transport drillers to and from their
rigs, and cat skinners to their cats. Three big D7 Caterpillars worked
together building miles and miles of muddy roads. Portable drills on steel
tracks followed behind. Hundreds of short holes were drilled into the
muck and muskeg, then stuffed with dynamite. The charges were set off

simultaneously and their echos were recorded on a seismic machine. If things looked promising, the big rigs would turn up after freeze-up and drill for oil.

It was a very long summer, but October finally came. Alders and birch trees were turning golden and the bugs were gone. I would be relieved in three weeks.

Like any new helicopter, the Jet Ranger had been plagued with problems all summer and we had already replaced a bad engine on this machine. Now the brand new one was once again whining like a cat with a foot on its tail.

"This engine is going to quit too," I told Ernie. I grounded the helicopter much to the consternation of the whole crew.

They were under intense pressure to finish this project before winter. In a panic, Klondike sent up Bob Evans, our top engineer. He and Ernie went over the helicopter with a fine tooth comb for hours. Bob finally stared doubtfully at me and said, "We can't find anything wrong with the engine. It's been a long summer for you. How are you standing up?"

"I'm fine," I replied, trying not to sound annoyed, "but that engine isn't!"

"The poor fricker's bushed. Needs time off," Ernie said in my defence with a sad hangdog expression on his face. *Damn,* I thought, *even my close friend Ernie thinks I've gone bonkers.*

"OK, let's take a test flight if you have the guts to sit in that thing with me," I replied, now even doubting myself. The three of us took off and flew a wide circle over the camp well clear of trees.

"There it is!" I shouted over the engine noise and the all-too-familiar whine. "This engine is going to fail soon!"

Even Ernie, my tried and true friend, gave me another doubtful look as I headed for the pad, landed and shut down. They simply hadn't heard the whine.

"I think you need a replacement, Hank. I'm going to talk to head office about this," Bob said, red-faced and angry. He headed for the radio telephone. Poor Ernie was beside himself. Never before had I tested his loyalty and mechanical genius to this extent.

He sidled up to me and whispered in my ear, "Look, mate, you think the fricken' helicopter is gonna quit then get your ass in there, start her up and hover 'til somthin' happens."

I climbed back into the helicopter and started it up. After about an hour, the oil pressure dropped to zero and the engine whine turned to a grinding sound. It was finally over.

I landed and shut down the now-smoking engine. I'd saved the company thousands of dollars and possibly a few lives, including mine. I was rewarded with a month off.

Two days later, after an all-night flight, the big Air Canada jet that I was on broke through the thin layer of cloud and Montreal appeared, stretching in all directions for miles.

The airplane flew over the narrow Jacques Cartier bridge and banked just enough that I could see the Expo site through the small window. Three long years before this when they were just starting construction I'd watched the event through the bubble of a CF-100 jet fighter. Jan was there in Montreal waiting for me. She had driven my car from Vancouver. We planned to visit Expo 67 then drive to Vancouver where she would catch a plane back to Australia.

We were very much in love, but had both finally agreed that it was the

Jet Ranger with failing engine.

best for both of us if we went our separate ways. We'd met in the wrong place at the wrong time. I wasn't ready to give up my flying adventures and she wasn't prepared to sit alone for months. I was coming off a bad marriage and she wanted a large family. After a wonderful visit at Expo we made the long drive to Vancouver. The last time I'd seen the Canadian prairies was through the sooty windows of a train when I travelled east to join the RCAF in August of '56. It was starker now. All the crops were harvested and the fields were covered with thousands of geese and ducks fuelling up on missed grain for the long trip south.

In a field in Alberta, I saw two Whooping Cranes standing in a patch of water, towering over the geese and ducks. A younger Crane stood between them. They had more than likely nested in Wood Buffalo National Park and were heading south for the winter. Their baby had survived.

CHAPTER TEN

A WOLF'S MOON

John Brock, the camp's chief prospector, kept me shivering on a craggy mountain until dusk while he pounded away at rocks with such heavy blows that even the bravest mountain sheep scurried for cover. A full year had passed since my meeting with the Mad Irishman in Earn Lake and I was back in the Yukon flying yet another Hiller 12E.

I'd spent a long day flying a gang of geologists, diamond drillers, and prospectors in and out of the camp to probe and drill the rocks for signs of precious metals as well as that famous Yukon gold. It had been a rough, windy day with snowflakes as big as Yukon black flies. The sky was starting to look like tar paper when we finally reached the camp, which was perched on a steep slope. A mean wind gusting down the draw made it hard to approach the small log helipad that stuck out precariously over a creek. After bouncing around, I finally got the helicopter onto the pad with a metallic crunch. Everything held together and I was very happy

Waiting for Brock
on a mountain top.

Landing on the log pad at the
camp at Quartz lake.

that this was the end of my flying day. John Brock sat stiffly in the seat beside me until I shut the machine down and the rotors came to a halt.

He looked more like an accountant with his pinched thin face, beak nose and round wire-rimmed glasses. But his face didn't have the pale, gaunt look of some city person. It was brown, weathered like leather and wrinkled like a man who spent a lifetime outside in the sun, wind and rain. Even with his guts rattled by the flight, I knew there was a barb coming my way. The smirk that passed for his smile was a dead giveaway.

"Flight skills in the toilet today, eh, Sands?" was his stab. Of course everyone else in the camp called me Hank, but not Brock. With that said, John took his pack sack and oversized rock hammer and headed down the slippery slope to the cook tent.

"Go sit on the sharp end of your rock hammer," I replied, too late for him to hear. John had a way of putting everything and everybody down. I slid my aching backside out of the chopper and considered kissing the ground.

"What crap did he lay on you this time?"

I jumped at the sound of Ernie Grant's voice behind me. I couldn't figure how he moved that huge body around so quietly. After he got my grumble for a reply, he began his nightly ritual of looking after the helicopter.

We shared a small, grubby, two-man tent set somewhat apart from the rest of the camp, but close the landing pad. Each time I took off, Ernie would have to endure blowing snow and woodstove ashes whipped up from the helicopter rotors. The tent camp was situated five miles upstream from Quartz Lake, a beautiful lake teaming with huge silver lake trout 40 miles east of the town of Watson Lake. All supplies were flown in by float plane to Quartz Lake and transported to the camp by helicopter. It was the middle of October and I had arrived here on the 15th of September 1968.

"You're my baby now," Ernie said as he tied down the main rotor so it wouldn't flap in the wind. He would be nursing the helicopter until it was too dark to see, and would be late for supper as usual.

The smell of fresh baked bread cheered me up and I headed for the cook tent as nimbly as those mountain sheep. Guy, our French cook, was a culinary genius. He'd given up a position as second chef at a famous

Ottawa hotel for the better pay offered in northern bush camps. The huge table was always heaped with vast bowls of meat, mashed potatoes, several kinds of veggies, salad, and even fresh baked pies. We were usually treated to a sit down affair complete with tablecloths. There were no cocktails or wine, but with a little imagination you could see yourself surrounded by red velvet and dark wood like at the Château Laurier. As I drew near, the wonderful smell of bread turned to the odour of garbage. The only thing that marred the whole dining experience was the smell of the dump site behind the cook tent.

The garbage oozed into the creek and headed down to Quartz Lake, a short distance away. The pristine lake was not only filled with trout, but also surrounded by shrubs and meadows teaming with countless furry and feathery creatures.

"Stinks out there," I said to John as I entered the tent. He sat at the head of the table, and just kept on eating, but the look he gave me was as cold as a witch's stare.

"The bloody thing won't start," Ernie grumbled, next morning. "It's too damn cold and look at all the ice on the rotors. Besides, all the rough landings you made yesterday have really buggered my baby this time."

There was no point in my taking exception to Ernie's liberal interpretation of yesterday's events, so I slunk off and left him to his engineering wizardry. Hours passed and even Ernie's ministrations with hammer and cuss words failed to get the Hiller 12E started. With cold fast approaching and the days getting shorter having no helicopter available was a disaster. Every morning and evening I would exchange the diamond drilling crew. Now the two men who had worked all night would have to continue slaving away until I could fly a fresh crew out.

And there was Brock to deal with! He was itching to beat away at more rocks with his oversized hammer. The whole crew of prospectors and drillers hung around the cook tent bored and bitchy. Guy served up an early supper which soothed them a bit. I hung around the helicopter and tried to help Ernie, but it didn't take a genius to see that I was just underfoot. Besides, the smell of steak being fried filled the air. I left the mad machinist and headed to the cook tent for dinner.

As I drew near I heard a munching sound. Even Brock didn't eat that loud, I thought. Then I nearly jumped out of my pants. Just a few feet from me was a huge black bear gobbling up the goodies that Guy had thrown down the slope. I'd seen lots of bears eating garbage in previous camps, but there was something different about this big fellow.

"Hi, Blackie," I said, as I walked close.

He looked up at me with almond eyes for just a moment, then returned to eating. I wasn't even sure the creature was a male, but he seemed to have a smile on his mug just like my crotchety Uncle Carl. He was certainly doing what we should have been doing, cleaning up the garbage.

"There's a bear out there," I said casually upon entering the cook tent. Brock's face turned red as a fire truck. He stabbed his fork into his steak, jumped up, rushed over to the tent flap, ripped it open and stared.

"Just our bloody luck, now we've got a Yukon black bear hangin' around and there's nothing meaner. Even grizzlies are afraid of 'em."

He glared at Guy and roared, "Feed this bloody steak to the bear. It'll kill him for sure."

"Hey cool yer jets a bit there, John boy," quipped Ernie as he entered the cook tent with tell-tale traces of grease still on his face and hands. Everyone quietly nodded their agreement.

"I've got dis apple pie dats magnific," Guy said, staring hopefully at Brock.

But Brock thrust all food aside, and rose to his full height, a good six feet plus. The gleam he always had in his eyes turned mighty evil, then demonic. We all knew we'd better listen to what he had to say.

"Mike and I were up in Ross River staking claims a couple years ago 'bout this time a year," Brock said. "A helicopter had dropped us off thirty miles from the nearest settlement.

"We staked all day and arrived back at camp damn tired and hungry. Only there wasn't any camp. A bloody bear had ripped the camp to pieces and ate everything in sight. He bit into all the canned stuff including a can of oil. That oil went right through him and he shat all over everything. I'm never goin' to forget that night. Couldn't even find a rabbit to eat. We ate scraps, spent a miserable night, and walked outta there next morning. In my opinion, the best bear is a dead bear."

With that he lapsed into silence and put a big piece of apple pie in his mouth. We all looked at one another and thought about that can of oil.

"Get this, Brock," I declared. "Last year at a camp in the oil patch they had six bears wandering around. None of them was causing us any trouble, but they shot them all anyway. Guess who had the job of getting rid of the rotting carcasses. Me! They simply tied a length of rope around a leg of the bear and put a loop at the other end. I was instructed to sling them off over the woods and drop them. I won't be doing that here unless this bear is a threat to us. So if you kill this bear, he'll be smelling a lot worse than that garbage in a week."

The chill in the already cold tent became frostier. John Brock just stared, and I suddenly realized, me a mere pup in the order of things in this camp must have sounded like a growling Pit Bull. Fortunately, I was the helicopter pilot and John Brock needed me desperately. I thought he was going to put me smartly in my place, but he just turned and stomped out.

The bear arrived every day on schedule. Since he was on his best behaviour, and doing a great job of cleaning up the garbage we all just let him do his thing. Except for Brock, of course, whose face became bleaker every time he saw that bear. When he started showing up around my tent to watch the munching bear, I knew he was up to something.

"What's up, Brock? Like the smell of things around here?" I asked on his third foray.

He ignored me.

The odour I referred to, trying to scare Brock off, was the smell of hot oil. Each night Ernie would drain the oil from the helicopter engine and put it on the tin heater in a big pot. It would simmer and boil like a malodorous stew all night and get poured back into the cranky beast in the morning. Usually, the bloody thing wouldn't start anyway, so Ernie would tease it to life with great quantities of hot water and the heat of a few cuss words.

After several days of nasty weather, a day dawned clear, warm and sunny. I was actually looking forward to a day of flying over this magnificent country until Ernie cornered me on our way back from breakfast.

"Maintenance night, mate, least two hours before dark an' sure could use some help."

I groaned inwardly.

Two hours before dark, I stood at attention beside the helicopter dressed in tattered coveralls ready to get covered in grease. Poor Ernie always paid a high price for my help though, as I always yapped away about anything and everything. No, it wasn't bitching. Good solid conversation, I called it. He had his little techniques to shut me up.

"You wanna get this helicopter put together before dark, hold on to that nut," Ernie growled. He applied pressure to the wrench. I kept talking and he added, "Blast, it ain't workin', go get me that left-handed monkey wrench."

I ignored his time worn joke, but I knew what he needed.

"Yeah, sure," I said. "But don't you want to hear the rest of my story first?"

He raised his eyes to heaven, and sighed mightily. I took no notice and hurried down towards the tent.

I was rummaging around in Ernie's cluttered tool box, when I caught the faint sound of rustling behind the tent. Must be the bear, I thought. I exited and rounded the tent very carefully.

And there stood Brock! He had an old army .303 rifle that had probably been his since WWII, and I had no doubt that he knew how to use it. I had to face the facts. My opinion wasn't worth two hoots to a bunch of prospectors so I simply stood and glared. Blackie arrived on schedule and began contentedly eating the day's menu. Brock levelled his rifle on the bear's heart with the poise of an experienced hunter. It never occurred to me that he would miss.

"Come on, Brock," I pleaded. "Blackie hasn't bothered anyone and we're moving the camp soon anyway."

Brock ignored me and fired.

I will never know if it was the slippery slope, a sudden gust of wind, or simply a mild-natured pilot gone mad, but down I went into John

Blackie the last time we saw him in daylight.

Brock with a crash. I think I saw the bullet remove a little fur from the bear's rump.

Blackie's eyes rounded with surprise and the permanent smile seemed to fade from his face. He vacated the scene promptly, but not without a final backward look that said, "You humans will pay for this!"

Brock turned slowly toward me and the look he gave me suggested that I might have to join the bear.

"Sorry, slipped," I said.

He stomped off mumbling something that sounded like, "Bears and idiot pilots."

That same night the bear visited us while we slept. Guy, who normally slept in a small tent attached to the cook tent, fled when he heard the sound of pots and pans rattling. Blackie was in the cook tent raising hell.

I remember waking up to the sounds of shouting and a shot or two, but no one was of a mind to take on that bear in the middle of the night. He managed to go through one end of that cook tent and out the other, leaving total devastation behind.

He returned the next two nights. Guy moved in with the

prospectors after Blackie's first nocturnal visit. Breakfasts were late and lacked variety. Everybody was madder than hell at the bear and I was definitely second on the hit list. I felt a little lower than the bear droppings left in the cook tent each night. Everyone treated me cordially, but I suspect that was because no one else knew how to fly the helicopter. What was I going to do to get off the hook?

"Watson Lake is only 40 miles away. Maybe the local game warden will lend us a bear trap?" I suggested.

The look Brock gave me made me decide that this just was a bad idea.

"We could situate a volunteer in the tent each night with a flare gun," was my next suggestion.

"And burn up my cook tent, eh," Guy quipped.

Anyway, no one volunteered to sit in that tent at night. Other ideas swilled in my head that didn't include bear traps and guns, but I sure wished I had some fireworks left over from Dominion Day, as Canada Day was called back then. But I didn't give up on churning out new ideas, each one crazier than the last.

Finally, I hit on a really bright idea. I announced it at breakfast, or what was left of breakfast after Blackie's nightly visit.

"Hey guys, why not hang a gas lantern over the dump at night to discourage the bear?"

"Humph," said Brock.

Everyone else looked at me like I was batty. But these were desperate times and I was on the spot to come up with something.

I figured there wasn't a tinker's chance in hell of it working, but the jury was on Brock's side. It was the bear's only chance.

That evening, I applied all of my brilliance and a little of Ernie's engineering talents to this task. We filled a large gas lantern to the brim with fuel, pumped it to bursting with air and hung it high over the garbage dump at nightfall.

I got up shortly after midnight to stoke the fire and add my auto-graph to the early snowfall that blanketed and made bleak beauty of the untamed Yukon forest. The creek gave off a slushy melody that mingled with the distant sound of a recently released Beatles song crackling out of a radio. A faint breath of wind stirred the weather-beaten Canadian flag that did double duty as a windsock. It hung precariously from a dead tree branch close to the helicopter.

It was bitter, cold outside, but I was more than curious to see what was going on. The lantern was still burning brightly. I saw a movement off in the distance.

"My god," I said to myself, "the bear's out there!"

I stood transfixed.

Suddenly John Brock appeared, striding out of the shadows cast by the lantern. Ah ha! I thought. The fool is pissing away the night, too.

Then I saw the dull glint of the rifle, held behind his back. The oaf was waiting for the bear to turn up in the light of the lantern. I saw the gleam in his eye. "Going to shoot something in the outhouse, Brock? Rats, maybe?" I said sarcastically.

We stared at one another across the snow.

In the end, I out-froze him. Blue and shivering, Brock retreated into his tent. I climbed eagerly into my Arctic 5 Star sleeping bag, and drifted off into a dreamless sleep for what seemed like mere seconds.

I woke up to the sound of howling!

"Jerkin' jets that sounds like it's right here in the tent," my oversized tent mate shrieked, struggling to get free of his Vietnam War surplus sleeping bag and knocking over the handmade table. Groggy from sleep, I felt my internal pilot panic button cut in. I dropped on hands and knees, groping forward in the dark for the tent opening. The howling grew in volume. Couldn't see a damn thing and the tent flap was welded with ice. I sensed Ernie's big frame behind me.

"Outta the way," Ernie shouted pushing me aside. He had the flap open in seconds and we ran out into the shadows cast by the lantern.

Off in the distance stood Brock, rifle pointed at the lantern. I floundered through the snow towards him. I wasn't going to let him shoot Blackie.

Strangely Brock and the men now emerging from the tents had their eyes fixed on the lantern, oblivious of me thrashing towards them. I slipped and fell flat on my face in the snow. Then I was up on hands and knees wiping snow out of my eyes. At last I turned and stared at the lantern.

There, in a chilling semi-circle around the burning gas lantern, stood a pack of wolves, eyes like hot coals and their shadows casting them into weird devil-like shapes on the glistening snow.

They sat howling at what they must have thought was the most brilliant full moon they had ever seen. Blackie was nowhere in sight, but I sensed his closeness.

No longer were any of us adversaries. We were men staring in silent awe at a rare spectacle.

Unlike coyotes who yap like dogs, these wolves seemed to be howling in perfect unison. Power and grace seemed to emanate from them.

Suddenly, the camp broke into bedlam. Pots and pans banged, shots were fired and men screamed like children. The wolves dissolved into the shadows like ghosts, and we all wondered, *Were they ever really there?*

"Dat's enough for me," Guy said next morning as we all sat around the breakfast table much the worst for wear. "You want a cook, 'Ank moves us outta dis 'ole."

"We move today," John Brock roared. "Crank up the helicopter, Hank!"

I couldn't believe it! This was the first time John Brock used my first name. The night's events had somehow brought a peace between us. There would be no rock pounding today. The whole crew would work every daylight minute to help with the move.

Even as I pushed the starter and heard the Hiller roar into life I saw the canvas being pulled from the tent frames. Men had already filled huge orange cargo nets with gear. Ernie stood holding the ring that held the net together. I hovered over to him and he attached the ring to the automatic hook under the helicopter. We both knew he would get a shock from the static electricity produced by the rotors, but we didn't care. Trip after trip, hour after hour, I moved nets and men to the new campsite down by Quartz Lake. The new camp was set up fast and efficiently.

It was almost dark when I approached and landed on the old pad for the last time. Ernie stood alone with our belongings at last ready to be piled into the helicopter. This strangely haunted place was now nothing but an ugly, empty space. The glistening snow of the night before was a mass of dirty footprints and black spaces where the tents once stood. I had no doubt that Blackie would soon arrive and eat what was left of the garbage. He would not be disturbed.

CHAPTER ELEVEN

CROSS ROADS

"Hey, waitress, get me another bloody beer," the scruffy looking miner yelled as he took another bite of his raw steak. It was one day before Christmas and the King Eddie restaurant was packed with a bunch of roughshod miners. I had the misfortune to be sitting next to this coarse, smelly oaf.

Suzy Cooper wasn't bothered a bit by obscenities. She simply smiled, hurried off and returned shortly with a big mug of beer which she set down in front of him. As she turned to go, he pinched her backside. Suzy was cute, but she was also a big strong girl. She turned like a tornado and knocked him right out his chair, flat on his back, out cold. The whole crowd roared with laughter.

Several weeks before this, I'd arrived once again in Stewart to relieve Bud Tipping. Suzy, Mrs. Hadley and Jim Waterford had welcomed me with open arms.

"Where's Jan?" they'd all asked. I will never forget the look of grief and shock on their faces when I tried to explain to them why she had returned to Australia. I wasn't even sure myself why she had left.

"Meet me in Spain in a year," had been her last words as she boarded the Quantas flight and headed for home.

"I should have hit him with a chair. That hurt!" Suzy said as she sat down beside me rubbing her bruised hand. Suzy Cooper was a fantastic waitress and we had become quite friendly. I ate all my meals in the restaurant and whenever she had a spare minute she'd sit with me and we'd make small talk.

She was waitressing up here to make enough money to return to university. Bud was back in town and I was free to go, but it had snowed for days and all flights had been cancelled.

"Do you want to spend Christmas with me?" Suzy asked. She stared at me with those lovely, hazel eyes and added, "Now that Jan's gone back to Australia, are you available?"

I was bowled over. In two sentences, Suzy had changed everything between us.

"Yes," I finally replied. It was time to move on. All the letters that Jan and I had been writing to one another had gradually dwindled to nothing.

On the morning of the 24th, there was 4 feet of fresh snow on the ground and the town was slowly digging out. The runway would not be plowed for two days. I was destined to spend Christmas in Stewart and now I was quite excited about it.

At 3 PM I was readying myself to go over to Suzy's when the phone rang. It was Bill Ross, who worked for Trans Provincial Airlines at the Stewart end of the Portland Canal. Bill was one of the best mechanic/

engineers on the west coast, albeit a little on the grumpy side. He did just about everything for the airline, including radio dispatch, baggage handling, and helping little old ladies on board the Goose aircraft.

"Better get your arse down to the dock fast. Paddy McNeil's there with a Goose waitin' to take you to Rupert. The sun's breakin' through, but we're expectin' more snow soon."

I'd forgotten that the Goose was amphibious. It didn't need the runway to land.

I rushed down to the restaurant. Suzy was cleaning up a table of dirty dishes. I told her that I was leaving.

"I know, I heard," she said with a sad look in her eyes. "See you next time."

I was at the dock in 20 minutes. I was the only passenger on board so once again I got to sit in the co-pilot's seat beside Paddy. He didn't need my help. The weather was good for the time being.

In Prince Rupert, I partied with Paddy and other fellow pilots and caught the 11 o'clock bus to Terrace. I arrived at my sister, Sylvia's place drunk with a broken bottle of red wine in my haversack.

Sylvia was a classic hell-raiser whose red hair matched the wine seeping out on the floor. When she wasn't singing and playing the guitar, or writing poetry she would be out in the forefront of some feminist demonstration throwing mud pies at politicians.

"I want you to meet my friend, Bonnie," she said as we hugged. Bonnie stood staring at the soaking haversack with a look on her face that suggested she wasn't really dying to meet me. That didn't last for long. She'd just broken up with her boyfriend. We were both on the rebound and in just a few days were attached to one another like magnets. In January, we took the CPR train to Edmonton and a bus to Calgary and began our nomadic life together. Bonnie simply was not prepared to spend months alone so we spent a long, cold winter together in a shoddy motel in High Level in Northern Alberta. After a short break, we spent an even longer hot summer in a shoddier motel in Steen River, a small trading post a few miles north of High Level. This was not the kind of life she had expected with me so once again I started thinking about a different career. When I explained my situation to Jim Lapinski, he had a very quick answer.

"Bud Tipping wants to get out of Stewart. The base is yours if you want it. You'll be home just about every night," he said.

I took him up on his suggestion with the speed of a bullet.

After what seemed like an eternity, I once again saw Stewart from the bow of the *Northland Prince* in the early morning mist. But this time, I had my automobile buried in its belly stuffed to the roof with all of our earthly belongings. Bonnie stood beside me excited and happy. We spent several days in the King Eddie then moved into the small company-owned house Bud had vacated.

Stewart had been an amazing boom bust town since Robert Stewart put his name to it in 1905. He was the towns first postmaster, and strangely had little to do with what made the town famous. Gold, silver, tons of less glamorous metals, and the men who searched for it are what put it on the map. Prior to the First World War, the population was 10,000 people. Towards the thirties it fell to a couple of dozen. Everyone called Stewart a town, but it was actually a city incorporated in 1930. It is nestled between mile-high Mount Dolly to the west and 7,000-foot Mt. Rainie on the east. The Portland Canal is its southern beach, and the rugged Bear Valley stretches to the north. The mountains on both sides of this wide valley

Stewart showing the old King Eddie Hotel (later destroyed by fire).

are full of tunnels that have produced thousands of ounces of gold and silver over the years. The early miners and prospectors, who dug out the ore with dynamite and pick axes, likely developed a taste for goat meat to survive, for there were hundreds of them clinging miraculously to the steep cliffs.

The 1968 there were no paved roads in or out. The closest town was Terrace. A very rough, gravel logging road ran from both towns to a wide river at Mezziadin Lake with no bridge. In summer, the best you could do was shout or wave at your Terrace neighbour while swatting mosquitoes. In winter, the road through the Bear Pass was absolutely impassable.

Stewart was in one of its many booms. The centre of activity was the

King Edward Hotel on the one main street. Ian McLeod, who also served as mayor, owned it.

All the touristy buildings of today were struggling businesses back then. The town was full of huge old empty hotels from the boom era. All were unsafe and fire hazards.

Two miles to the south was the town of Hyder, Alaska, boasting three bars and a population of about 28 people. It was the only American town totally dependent on Canadian utilities and tourist dollars. There was no Canadian customs office. Everyone in Stewart had a mailbox in Hyder, a Sears Roebuck USA account and enjoyed duty-free delivery of almost everything, but cars. Booze flowed as freely as the glacier-fed rivers. Pure grain alcohol called Alcool was available for a stipend. It was also liberally administered to tourists. A two-ounce shot glass full of the fiery liquid was placed under your nose on your first visit. You either tossed it down or left the town in shame. As you drank it, tears ran down your face and you fought for breath. Everyone in the place clapped and slapped you on the back.

You'd been *Hyderized!* The old alcoholic bartender and owner of the Glacier Inn loved to slip an ounce or two into the weak American beer. Many tourists and more than a few of the locals were carried out of that bar.

The telephone system in both towns was out of the dark ages. Everyone had a crank telephone and everyone could hear what everyone else was saying. Millie, the lone telephone operator, was also the town gossip. The telephone office was open from 8 AM to 5 PM Monday to Friday. After that all communication with the outside world was cut off, other than a somewhat unreliable radio in the police station in case of emergencies. If you wanted to know what went on in town you would simply go to the King Eddie bar at 5:05 and buy Millie a beer.

It snowed so much in Stewart that snow plows were largely useless. In the fall all road names and stop signs were removed so they wouldn't get chewed up by the huge snow blowers. The blowers augured up the snow and blew it over what sometimes were 10 foot walls of crisp snow onto people's yards. Even though they tried to plow in the darkness during the wee hours to avoid people and animals, there were a few late night casualties, none human, thank goodness.

In the spring of 1969 the Granduc contract came to an end and Klondike had no interest in keeping a helicopter in Stewart. But Bonnie and I sure didn't want to leave.

"I can make a living here without the contract," I told Jim Lapinski over the phone.

Jim reluctantly gave in and I did fine until Vancouver Island Helicopters, based out of Victoria, moved one of their helicopters into town to compete with me through the summer. Competition might be a good thing, but not in Stewart on a quiet year. We were both barely getting enough flying to pay for the gas. Jim Lapinski phoned me July 19th. I was home that day because the weather was awful and no one was flying anywhere.

"We have a job for you in Dawson Creek with an oil company for the rest of the summer," he said. "We want you to fly over there tomorrow."

I was flabbergasted!

"If I leave, Vancouver Island Helicopters will take over all my flights and we'll be finished here," I said desperately.

"Sorry, but we have to go where the money is," was his gloomy reply.

"We'll relieve you in Dawson Creek in a couple of weeks so you can go back to Stewart and pack up your things."

I went looking for Peter Corley Smith and finally found him at the airport. He was the Vancouver Island helicopter pilot, and we had been friendly competitors all summer. I found him at the airport, explained the situation and turned over all the flights that I had booked to him.

"Look, Hank," he said. "Why don't you give Alf Stringer a call. I'm going back to university in September and you could take over from me."

Alf, an engineer by trade, was now president and owner of Vancouver Island Helicopters. He and helicopter pilot Carl Agar had founded Okanagan Helicopters way back in the '50s. I took Peter's advice and phoned Alf.

"We want to set up a base in Stewart," he said, "but we have to offer the job to one of our own pilots."

I left for Dawson Creek the next morning, leaving Bonnie behind to start packing. True to his word, Jim sent a pilot to relieve me two weeks later and I returned to Stewart, leaving the helicopter behind. Once again, Bonnie and I were at loose ends. Our life together in Stewart was over. Our destination was Klondike Helicopters home base in Calgary.

On a sunny Saturday morning in late August, we had our belongings packed in shipping crates outside the old rental home and sat unhappily on the steps waiting for the moving truck.

We would follow it through town for the last time and once again watch everything being loaded on the *Northland Prince*. The phone rang in our house, which surprised me, because it was supposed to have been cut off. I picked it up on the fourth ring. It was Alf Stringer calling from Victoria.

"The base is yours if you want it, Colonel," he said. "None of our pilots want to move up there. You can take over from Peter on September 6th."

I was to learn later that Alf called everyone *Colonel*.

Oh, I wanted it alright. I was so excited I didn't hear the truck pulling up outside. They were already loading boxes when I finally got off the phone and tripped down the steps shouting, "Stop! Stop!"

We began loading all our stuff back into the house. Peter turned up that evening with a bottle of wine and a brand spanking new hat with the initials VIH on it. I would have it beaten up in no time, with a nice ring of sweat around the band. Peter looked and spoke more like an English gentleman than a lowly helicopter pilot. Once settled into chairs around a still unpacked box, we sipped wine and recounted the summer's adventures. We were on the same team now.

The funniest story Peter had to tell was the time he flew BC's Honourable Minster of Highways on a road tour up in the Mezziadin Lake area.

"The bugger spat on the floor of the helicopter. I told him if he ever did that again he could bloody well walk home."

That was Peter for you.

Bonnie and I soon purchased an old house that had been pre-built in Vancouver BC.

It had been barged in and set up in 1928 as Stewart's railway station house and later moved onto a lot in town. The house creaked in the wind, but I knew it could withstand a hundred feet of snow without flinching.

Huge bolts held steel-hard fir beams so firmly together they'd probably last for a thousand years. When I didn't have the helicopter's controls in my hands, I had a hammer and saw. The house needed a lot of fixing, but it was our first real home.

Old Jim Waterford, in his capacity as town agent, had the pleasure of marrying us and assisting us in adopting a 3-month-old baby we named Henry. We lived in Stewart for three more event-filled years.

CHAPTER TWELVE

ALL'S WELL THAT ENDS WELLS

"Hey, Hank, you busy?" Bill Ross shouted over the telephone. It was snowing so heavily outside that even the ravens weren't flying. I was busy fixing the toilet in my old house. I certainly wasn't planning on doing any flying today.

"We just got an emergency radio call from Ron Wells at Mess Creek. His radio was all broken up. Then we lost him."

"What do you mean, we lost him?" I replied, heart stuck in my larynx.

"He said his engine had quit and he was going down. Didn't sound too worried, but you know Ron, always cool as a glacier."

"Yes, cool," I said.

Ron was a fellow fixed-wing pilot and good friend.

"Think you could spare the time to go have a look? There isn't anything else flyin' from here to the North Pole today," he added, sounding like he was asking me out for a beer.

"See you at the helipad in about 20 minutes," I said.

"Dammit!" I thought to myself. "The only way we can reach Mess Creek on a day like this is through the Bear Pass." This was the last thing I wanted to do, but I washed the odorous sewer guck off my hands while my wife whipped up a lunch.

It was late morning on 25th March. The Trans Provincial Airlines office was a mere 200 feet from my new half-built hanger. When I arrived, Bill was already there shovelling a way out for the helicopter. We soon had the two-passenger Bell 47 B1 out of the hanger, fuelled and ready.

We took off and headed north following the rough gravelled, nearly-arrow-straight road that cut through the meandering Bear River Valley. The road and primitive log bridges always needed repairing as the river was prone to flooding. They were once part of the railroad bed for the Portland Canal Short Line Railway which was built in the '20s.

The rail had run 12 miles north from Stewart to a proposed mine called Red Cliff. The original plan was continuing to build the railroad east through the Bear Pass, then north to the rich coal fields at Groundhog Mountain about 100 miles from Stewart.

But it never got finished. Two things probably killed the dream. First, building a railway through the awesome Bear Pass would be a costly nightmare. Second, the Great Depression was soon to happen.

The old railroad bed was just about all we could see in the heavy snowfall. Wet snow clung like a big white circle on the bubble and the helicopter humped like a camel as the ice built up on the rotors only to be thrown off by the twisting, bending and rippling blades. Once we entered the Bear Pass the heavy wet snow gradually turned dry and hard. Gut-wrenching, gusting headwinds tore at us and slowed us to a turtle's pace. No other living creature inhabited this 30-mile-long pass in late March,

Strohn Lake and the Bear Glacier in summer.

not even the mountain goats. Mile-high avalanche paths lined both sides of this incredibly steep valley, waiting only for some noise or vibration like a helicopter to send thousands of tons of snow cascading down at lighting speed. If the snow didn't bury us, wind gusts created by the avalanche could tear us to pieces and in this weather we wouldn't see it coming. The huge Bear Glacier finally loomed in front of us. Blue ice as high as an apartment block bottomed out on frozen Strohn Lake. A mere 20 years ago, this glacier had filled the whole valley, and the lake had been dammed by the ice. Known as a *Jökulhlaup* in Icelandic, this formation behaved like a flushing toilet. As the lake filled up with water, the huge icebergs began to float, sending the icy waters roaring down the narrow valleys causing massive damage all the way to Stewart. Once the water was drained, the icebergs re-plugged the opening and waited patiently for the lake to re-fill and repeat the whole cycle again. Strohn Lake did this five times in recorded history and probably hundreds of times before that. When I arrived in 1967, the glacier had retreated far enough that the lake was no longer dammed. The gravel road that was cut through a sheer cliff opposite the glacier was buried under tons of snow and barely visible.

Finally, Mezziadin Lake appeared in the distance, frozen solid and covered with several feet of snow. We were at last clear of the pass and hoped it would be clear sailing from here on.

There wasn't a breath of air and the outside air temperature gauge read a full 30 degrees colder than Stewart. The sun was breaking through the haze. Moose browsed everywhere on the edges of the lake. A pack of grey wolves fed on a carcass less than 50 feet from a big bull laying out on the snow sunbathing himself, not seeming to care about their presence or their activity.

We turned north and were soon flying in snow showers again, but it was nothing like it had been in the Bear Pass. Between the two of us, with much map folding and a few wrong turns, Bill and I finally made it to Mess Creek, at the bottom of a wide valley where trees barely poked above the snow and blue glaciers hugged the craggy mountains on each side. Our search began.

"There it is, dead ahead!" Bill shouted suddenly, pointing.

Sure enough there sat the 10-passenger, single-engine de Havilland Otter off in the distance, its tail buried in at least 10 feet of snow. We landed as close as we could get to the downed aircraft. The only movement inside or out was the rocking of its wings as our rotors blasted them with hard granules of powder snow. Once I got the helicopter firmly settled up to its belly in snow, I turned the engine off. There was no movement from the Otter for what seemed like the longest time. Finally, the Otter's hatch wiggled a little and opened, and there stood Ron Wells. He looked like he was on his way to church.

"Hi folks," he said in a mellow voice, as he scrambled towards us up to his waist in snow, and clambered into the helicopter beside us.

"Sure nice of you to come up here. Sorry to put you to all this bother. Now let's see. We have a bit of a problem here. There's five of us on board plus you two which makes a total of seven. Hmmm, too late to get all of us out of here before dark," he added as an after thought.

Ron looked more like a banker than a pilot, but bright braces holding up baggy pants didn't do much for the banker look. He was pushing 60, with beer bottle glasses and a hearing aid stuck in his left ear.

"I haven't got time to listen to you two talk about the weather," Bill said grumpily. "Fill me in on what that engine did that brought you down into this pile of snow, and I'll go have a look. You two pilgrims can figure out what you're gonna do with those people on board."

"Well, let's see now," Ron replied. "The engine didn't actually quit, but it sure sputtered and backfired and lost all its power. I headed for this clearing and set her down best I could."

"Hummmff," was all we got from Bill as he clambered out of the helicopter. The deep snow hid the limp from his arthritic leg as he headed straight for the airplane, and started pulling cowlings off the engine.

"I'd rather be fixing that engine than trying to figure what to do with those people staring out the Otter windows at us," I said.

Ron and I sat in the helicopter, since it was the only decent place to sit, and started planning.

"Well, Hank," he said matter-of-factly, "on board I've got Doctor

Wilson and Nelly Tillie, the government nurse from Telegraph Creek. She came along to look after Suzy Jack, and help the doctor who's got a bad heart. Suzy's got a cast from toe to hip, multiple fractures you know. Oh, just about forgot Harry. He's a friend of mine who came along for the ride."

"Let me get this straight, Ron," I replied. "You've got a sick doctor, a woman in a cast, a nurse, and a friend sitting in that plane, and we're 50 miles from the nearest settlement which happens to be Telegraph Creek, sitting on 10 feet of snow two hours before nightfall."

I didn't bother to add that I was low on fuel, and it was growing colder as winter shadows crept across the snow-covered desolation.

"Shaft Creek's only 10 minutes flying from here," Ron said calm as a cucumber. "Seems we'd be better off over there. At least we'd have a roof over our heads. Might even be some food. Got any fuel nearby?"

He'd read my thoughts.

"Yep, in Shaft Creek. All we have to do is find it somewhere in the snow," I replied.

Shaft Creek, just 10 miles away, was separated from us by a half-mile high pass that was nothing more than a ridge of rock that probably supported a glacier not too long ago.

The permanent campsite was built close to what was purported to be a vast ore body of copper. Numerous trailer units had been flown in by large helicopters and attached to one another. I'd flown in and out of the camp many times during the summer and once this winter to check for snow damage. In the summer the mine site was bustling with a hundred men with warm beds, and food to die for. Now it would be buried in snow and devoid of all life.

Though the last ice age had left this valley thousands of years ago, a glacier must have covered the campsite until a few hundred years ago. It was as treeless and desolate as the moon.

"Sounds like it's the best option," Ron said. "I sure don't want to spend a night in the Otter."

We went over to the airplane and told the folks the good news.

"How are we going to get Suzy in that little helicopter?" Nellie asked.

Ron and I looked at one another. She'd picked up on a question that was on both our minds.

While everyone scrambled to get organized for a helicopter ride, Ron tried the radio one more time. Through squeaks, squeals and lots of static, he managed to tell the base that we were going to Shaft Creek and were anxiously waiting to be picked up.

The last thing the dispatcher in Terrace said was, "We'll be out to get you when the weather gets better."

"Bring food," Ron shouted.

I didn't think they heard him. Static won the battle.

Each trip we'd be a little overweight, especially with our patient who looked like she weighed at least 200 pounds, before adding the weight of the cast. We sure didn't have the same problem the crew of the *Titanic* had trying to decide who went first. We needed muscle and brain to figure a way into that buried camp. Ron and his big burly friend, Harry, were the best we could come up with so I stuffed them into the helicopter and headed for Shaft Creek. It turned out that Harry was a meteorologist. I kinda figured that out as he talked a lot about the weather as we skimmed over the pass.

The snow gods had been kind to us. Both the entrance to the cookhouse and the fuel cache had been blown clear by the fierce winds in this valley.

"I'll poke around and see what I can get going," was the last thing Ron had to say before I dumped the two of them unceremoniously beside the cookhouse and headed back for more people. As I landed back at the Otter, Bill glared at me for daring to disturb his intense inspection of the big radial engine. But when he saw us dragging Suzy Jack towards the helicopter like a sack of potatoes, he hobbled over and took charge. Loading things into aircraft was his specialty.

"If we can't get ya inside the cabin we're going to tie you on the rack just like they do in the *M.A.S.H.* TV show," Bill said seriously. "You seen that show?"

Poor Suzy looked at him from her sitting position in the snow, rolled her eyeballs in fear and screamed something in her native tongue.

"Guess maybe you have seen that show so we'll get you in the cabin somehow. Even if we have to cut a hole in the bubble," was Bill's say on the matter.

Now it was my turn to stare at him and roll my eyeballs. It was a little like trying to stuff a walrus into a sardine can, but we managed to drag her into the cabin and slide her along the seat. Her head was hanging out the other door before we got her body inside. The cast ended up hard against the inside of the bubble where it left a permanent scratch.

We pulled the terrified woman as upright as we could, leaving just enough room for me to fly and for Nurse Tillie to squeeze in beside her. Fortunately, Nelly Tillie was a small woman. Thankfully we were able to strap their belongings on the racks outside, instead of Suzy. I was off again for Shaft Creek.

Ron and Harry were there to help with the unloading, so I wasted no time getting back to Mess Creek for the final load. It was starting to snow again.

I hustled Bill and my last passenger into the chopper and opened the throttle full bore. Visibility in the snow was practically down to zero and I barely made it over the snow-covered pass this time. It took me till dark to get the machine re-fuelled and settled in for the night.

Smoke billowed out of the chimney and lights came on almost simultaneously inside the cookhouse telling me that they'd got the generator going.

Fortunately, the cookhouse and some of the sleeping quarters were all under one roof, although we had to dodge beams that had been installed every few feet to hold the roof up over winter. Blankets, sheets and pillows were stored in waterproof boxes. We had everything we needed, except running water and decent food. A long row of toilets and sinks stood useless. We put garbage bags in the toilets and melted great pots of snow for water.

"Got the furnace working and supper's on the way," Ron shouted with glee as I entered the now almost warm cookhouse.

"What's for supper?" I asked, not knowing what if any food had been left behind.

"Fried bully beef. Found a whole case of canned meat and several boxes of Corn Flakes. Don't know how to cook the flakes so we'll have 'em for breakfast."

"Any milk?" I joked.

The mean night wind that beat at us was muffled by the deep snow on the roof, and over most of the windows. It was going to be a long night.

Bill shuffled around the place fixing this and that, and got the batteries to the single-side-band radio charging up. Hopefully, we'd have communication with the outside world in the morning. Certainly we needed a more reliable radio than the one in the Otter.

Ron and Harry found a deck of cards with a missing deuce. The joker became the deuce at the stroke of a pen. The rest of us drifted off in pairs.

Doctor Wilson, a kindly white-haired gent, told me how he was retired, and had flown up here as a favour to Nelly. He and Suzy, who were both exhausted, went to bed early. Nelly and I talked well into the night.

"I'm from Sheffield, England," she told me after explaining she'd emigrated from Britain a year ago, and had taken up residence in Telegraph Creek to build a career in Canada.

My great-great-grandfather was mayor of Sheffield," I replied, glad that we'd broken the ice. I told her how my father had come to Canada in the '20s from England. His accent today was as pure as Nellie's.

"After spending a year in Telegraph Creek, taking care of the native population, today's events haven't ruffled a single feather in my cap," she added, "but I could have managed a lot easier if I was wearing a pair of pants instead of this silly skirt."

The weather was clear and a little below freezing in the morning. We discovered that corn flakes and water aren't very appetizing, so most of us had more fried bully beef again for breakfast.

Common sense says that helicopters are a piece of machinery with no feelings. I'm just not sure about that. I felt as close to this helicopter as a cowboy would feel about his horse if he'd spent as many hours mounted on it as I had. Today it was behaving like a mule. It gave one big burst then ignored my persistent cranking. At this temperature any car in the world would start immediately, but not these Texas-born helicopters.

Bill came wandering over with two big pieces of sheet metal.

"Found these in the workshop. They should do fine," he said.

"For what?" I asked.

"We're gonna light a fire under this stubborn helicopter's ass. Only way we're gonna get her started."

I wondered what my engineer friend, Ernie, would have thought about this idea.

Bill placed one of the pieces of metal on the snow, and the other over a bed of dismantled bone-dry crates. I'd heard of this being done, but it sure wasn't something you mentioned to your boss.

After a nervous 20 minutes I was very happy to help Bill snuff out the fire with snow The somewhat-warmed machine still wouldn't start. Bill got out his tool kit, grumbled something, and began poking around the engine.

"Hit her now," he shouted. The sharp smell of starting fluid filled the air. Starting fluid, which is nothing more than ether, may put people to sleep, but it wakes up cold engines in a hurry. I hit the starter and the helicopter started with a cloud of smoke and a roar.

At this same moment, a brilliant red airplane appeared over the ridge between us and Mess Creek. I'd never seen an all red airplane other than at air shows and almost expected to see a leather helmet and long white scarf flying out behind. Unlike Mess Creek, the wind-whipped snow on the runway here was hard packed, making for perfect landing conditions. The Red Baron made a nice ski landing right beside the helicopter and pulled close. The pilot clambered out and was about to introduce himself when Ron stuck his head out from the cook shack where we'd left him to organize our guests and do the dishes.

"Ralphy, my boy!" he shouted at the pilot as he ran towards us full bore. I'd never seen him this excited. He must have turned the dishwashing over to someone else. After much handshaking and backslapping, we all got down to the business at hand.

"I can take the passengers and all their gear with me to Terrace," Ralph said, "but what about the three of you?"

He meant Bill, Ron and I. We had already discussed this over coffee. Our plan was to head back to the Otter and find out what the heck was wrong with it.

"While you mutts slept, I got the camp radio going," Bill growled. "I'll call in for parts if I can ever figure out what the hell's wrong with that bloody engine and we need blasted food."

I don't know if it was that engine problem, or too much bully beef, but Bill was definitely a little more grouchy than usual this morning.

We loaded the nurse, doctor, patient and everyone else on board the airplane. Ralph took off with ease on the hard-packed snow and did a quick low flypast. Happy hands waved at us from the windows. Now it was time for us to get to work.

The three of us jumped into the helicopter, and headed for the Otter. While Bill worked on the engine, Ron and I built a runway. The soft snow had to be trampled down to improve the chances of the Otter taking off. And it had to be done wearing snowshoes, stomp after stomp, foot after foot.

When our legs were too tired to do any more, Bill handed us shovels and said, "Maybe you could do a little digging around the Otter. You know, give your legs a rest, then go back to making me a runway."

We followed orders as best we could.

"I've found the problem," Bill finally shouted from a distance. We slowly slogged back to the Otter. As we shuffled in close, the big smile and gleam in his eye told us that Bill was going to be happy for a while at least.

"See this," he said like a professor to his students. "This is a rocker arm. It's broken."

We both knew what a rocker arm was, but we maintained our silence.

"Had me fooled. Took a compression tests and all was normal. Exhaust valve was stuck closed and all the gases backed up into the intake manifold and strangled your engine good. Never heard of one of these breakin'. You two ever heard of one these breakin'?"

"No, no," I said.

"Me neither," Ron said.

"OK," Bill barked, "let's head over to Shaft *toot sweet* so I can order the parts that I need. If we're lucky they'll get over here before dark. I'll have you guys outta here by tomorrow noon, provided you build that blasted runway a little faster."

Ron and I grinned at one another. We were getting off work early today.

After the parts were ordered and more begging for food we began the long wait, praying that the good weather would hold. We heard the drone of the airplane long before we saw it. The pilot landed pretty much in the same spot as the Red Baron had.

There wasn't much daylight left, so he quickly dropped equipment and food supplies in the snow, took off and headed back to Terrace. Bill sorted through the parts, while Ron and I attacked the food supply. It was like Christmas. The good Samaritans had sent steaks, bacon and eggs with all the trimmings and whiskey.

Ron cooked up that steak so fast that we were stuffing our faces before Bill had even sorted out the parts. Even the bottle of whiskey had to wait until our bellies were full.

Next morning, we dined on bacon and eggs, and headed for Mess Creek at first light. We left the dishes for the spring clean-up crew. We all wanted the heck out of this place. True to his word, Bill had the engine back together at noon. Ron and I spent the morning, once again, stamping the snow with snowshoes. When finished, we were nearly ready for crutches.

"Hit her," Bill shouted. The motor cranked over, slowly and grudgingly. Then it sputtered. We were thinking about building a fire under it when the big radial engine roared to life, kicking, jerking and belching out clouds of smoke.

After a while it ticked over perfectly.

"See you in Stewart," Bill shouted above the din, and climbed aboard.

I think he would have preferred to ride back with me, but engineers have a code among themselves. After they fix it, they ride on the first test flight. This makes us pilots feel confident in their work. This wasn't just an ordinary test flight. This was a one-shot deal!

I could see Ron in the cockpit. The ready smile was gone as he added power. When we were stomping out the snow the field looked huge. Now it looked small and the trees at the end tall and unforgiving.

The big radial engine was close to full throttle. Snow blasted the shuddering wings and tail, but the aircraft didn't budge. It looked like we'd be doing more digging and praying. I heard more power being added, probably over the limit. The noise was horrendous!

The big bird suddenly popped out of the hole and lumbered along the man-made runway, rapidly closing on the trees.

Just before it was too late, it finally lifted into the air and climbed, so close to the treetops that they shook violently in the airplane's wake. The airplane made a wide turn and roared towards me at treetop height. Ron waved and dipped his wings in a time-honoured pilot's salute then climbed slowly out of sight.

I stood beside the helicopter and enjoyed the absolute silence. It was awesome. No birds or other creatures were moving in this place at this time of year and no breeze rustled the trees.

I dallied a while because total silence is a nice thing for a pilot to hear. Then, I headed for Stewart. The weather was much better than it was during the trip in, so, in no time, I was back in my train station house, working on the plumbing.

This is the helicopter I used to rescue Ron Wells, sitting in front of a hundred-year-old cabin in Alaska. Although not mentioned in this book, I flew many prospectors in and out of Alaska.

CHAPTER THIRTEEN

AVALANCHE CONTROL

" "A better name for us would be 'Avalanche Out of Control Team'," Marty said, when we were having a beer at the King Eddy. He'd had a frustrating day fighting avalanches that had closed the road once again between Stewart and the mine at Tide Lake.

"It's like spraying water on aphids," was his next comment after a deep suck on his beer. "We've recorded close to a thousand inches of snow at the mine site."

"Didn't know you knew anything about gardening," I said jokingly. "Should be good growing weather tomorrow. It's supposed to be sunny for a change."

Marty gave me that 'what are you talking about' look, and pressed on.

"OK, if it is good flying weather, we've got to fly to Leduc tomorrow. They're worried about the tunnel opening gettin' buried by an avalanche so we're going to do some bombing."

The closed camp at Leduc.

It was 1969. Granduc had finally opened its 11-mile-long tunnel from Tide Lake to Leduc making travel to and from Leduc little more than a subway trip. The camp itself was perched precariously on a small flat of land about one-half mile from the tunnel opening, right below an avalanche path. After an avalanche killed 26 men there on February 18, 1965, Granduc hired a team to do battle with the endless snow that gravity sent crashing down the steep slopes. The camp was still used in the summer, but no one lived there in the winter as the company was not prepared to lose any more men. Nevertheless, both the buildings and the tunnel opening a short distance away were both in dangerous avalanche paths and needed to be protected. Men and equipment were constantly moving in and out of the tunnel opening. Now the biggest risk to life was the 32-mile road between Stewart and Tide Lake.

The precious copper ore was processed at the mine site at Tide Lake and trucked to Stewart for shipment by huge freighters to locations around the world. Tons of dynamite had been used to etch this road into the side of a mountain that was avalanche hell. For years, the company was content to hire part-time men in the autumn to fight these avalanches. Most of them left in the spring to go mountain climbing or some other crazy adventure. But the battle against ice and snow would never be over.

Finally, this year they'd hired Marty Coolidge, who was on a year-round salary. His one and only job was to control those dangerous avalanches and keep track of his part-time crew of wanderers.

I woke early next morning, crept to the east window so as not to wake up my wife, and peeked out through the curtain. It was one those rare sky blue winter days. Mt. Rainie, named after an early prospector, supported a sheer, glistening blue glacier that ever threatened to bury Stewart. It would hold off the sun until almost eleven o'clock. Foxtails of snow whisked off its 7000-foot-high peaks, indicating it was quite windy up there.

Marty and I would be taking off at noon and would probably fly until sunset, which happened early in these deep valleys. We always planned our bombing runs as late as possible in hopes that what little warmth we had from the sun would loosen up the slopes a little.

I had the Bell 47 B2 turbo-charged helicopter up and running when Marty arrived at noon. This was a wide cabin version of the old *M.A.S.H.* machine with a few extra inches of space for large bottoms.

Marty wasn't a big man and the huge packsack full of dynamite, a mile of fuse, and the ever-sensitive blasting caps that he carried, made him look even smaller.

We took off over the Portland Canal and headed for Hyder. A weather-beaten sign with *Friendliest Ghost Town in Alaska* written on it hung over a rock cairn that marked the Canada-US border. Swans and Canada geese on the inlet crowded around old ice-covered pilings which once supported a turn-of-the-century steam train. Some thought that the train was still down there in the mud. Even at this early hour, a couple of people were heading into the Glacier Inn, one of the towns bars that never closed.

We flew following Granduc's road north. Mile-high Mount Dolly rose majestically on our right. The Canada-US border was a wide cut in magnificent stands of spruce, which faded into white obscurity above the tree line. The Premier Mine site, once one of the world's richest gold mines, stood stark and deserted on our right while the roaring Salmon River gushed out of an enormous blue ice cave at the foot of the Salmon Glacier and ate away at the road. The road skirted west and climbed sharply up the side of an almost treeless mountain that looked like a big mound of ice cream with the road a mere trickle of chocolate syrup running through it.

Just below the road, the vast glacier extended as far as the eye could see. In the summer, it was covered with dirt and gravel and the dangerous blue crevasses were exposed. Now it was a frozen, static river. We climbed steeply to keep above it.

Summit Lake appeared in the distance. Like Strohn Lake in the Bear Pass, this three-mile-long lake had also experienced a *Jökulhlaup* the previous summer. The Salmon Valley below had been flooded all the way to Stewart, severely damaging Granduc's precious road. I had spent several

Summit Lake above the Salmon Glacier.

days moving men and equipment at a washed-out section near Hyder. Now the icebergs sat like enormous ice cubes on the empty lake bottom.

Right above the lake on one of the few outcroppings on the road sat an ex-military 3.5-inch rocket launcher. It looked like an oversized astronomical telescope. But this launcher was a dangerous weapon firmly mounted on a concrete pad. It was always pre-aimed at the enemy, a mile-long avalanche path. It would be fired by a carefully trained crew on warmer days when wet snow, rain or fog turned the steep slope into an unstable, invisible, treacherous killer. There was also a truck-mounted launcher nearby.

The glacier became even steeper and meandered like a frozen river to its summit. I had to make numerous tight turns to gain height and avoid the perpetual downdrafts. Mountain goats clambered about in ledges

Summer picture of Salmon Glacier,
showing Granduc's hazardous road
and the Salmon River which had
flooded weeks before.

At right, road sign to Hyder.

barely wide enough to hold a rabbit. I gave them a wide berth, as I had
learned from past experience, that they were terrified of helicopters and
were inclined to jump recklessly if we got too close.

"What's that?" Marty shouted, pointing at a dark spot right in the
middle of the all white glacier. I flew over to take a look. A lone wolverine

stared at us with a 'What are you doing here' look. Then the tough, mean little critter simply ignored us and continued walking.

Finally, we were at the crest of the glacier flying close to the snow at over 7,000 feet. Black craggy mountains still rose vertically thousands of feet on each side of us. The winds were always fierce and unpredictable in this foreboding pass. As we entered into the Leduc Valley, a sudden updraft hit us and we went up like a rocket. The rotors shuddered and the RPM dropped to a dangerous low speed. The blood was forced out of our heads and pooled in our feet.

"I'm gonna shit my pants!" Marty yelled.

We had risen 1,500 feet before I could react. Now, we were above even the highest peaks.

I felt like I was sitting on the edge of a skyscraper with my feet dangling into space. Marty looked as white as the glacier, but his bowels remained intact.

I tried reducing power and the helicopter still hung suspended by the updraft, which was also throwing us about like a dead leaf in a whirlwind. I bottomed out the collective to put the helicopter into autorotation and that's how we finally descended into the valley.

In summer, the Leduc Valley looked like it was the surface of the moon. Miles of grey rock etched and carved by very recent glaciers supported few trees or shrubs. In this foreboding valley it rained all summer, and snowed hundreds of inches all winter. Now everything was a white moonscape.

The outlet from the tunnel was kept ploughed. Fresh rock tailings that had been recently dumped stood out in sharp contrast to the rest of the valley which looked like a carved-out version of the arctic tundra. The buildings in the camp looked like snow-covered tree stumps.

The updraft had unravelled us. At this point, I think the two of us wanted to land at the tunnel, shut the helicopter down and ride the tunnel train back to Tide Lake, but there was work to do.

Miles of steep and dangerous avalanche paths topped with cornices 50 feet in height needed to be bombed. It was about as safe as flying a load of bombs over Berlin in World War II with wings full of holes and a dead engine or two.

Marty was finally back to the calm, cool collected kind of man needed for this kind of work. He wrapped a bundle of dynamite with duct tape, inserted a blasting cap and wound several feet of fuse around the sticks. We flew up and over a vast potential avalanche path above the tunnel opening and came to a shaky hover over a huge cornice.

A snow cornice is an overhanging edge of hard wind-packed snow on the ridge or the crest of a mountain. Fashioned by strong winds and blowing snow, they usually form on the leeward sides of mountains and often look like a big wave on a surf beach just before it breaks. Cornices are very dangerous. They can break off and trigger massive avalanches as they crash into the fragile layers of snow on the steep slopes below them. They are particularly vulnerable to collapse during periods of warm, wet or sunny weather.

It was unlikely that the cornice we were hovering over at this moment was going to break off today, so we intended to give it a little help.

Marty lit the fuse. Acrid smoke filled the cabin as it hissed rapidly towards the blasting cap.

"Easy as peein' in a toilet," Marty shouted as he opened the helicopter

Rocket Launcher and crew parked directly above Summit Lake, and
the two mountains and the high pass through to Leduc Camp.

door, leaned out and tossed the sticks smoothly onto the top of the cornice
where it rolled a bit and stopped. Clouds of smoke curled up as the hot
fuse met the ice and cold air.

"Get the hell out of here!" he shouted.

I didn't have to be told twice. Two to three feet of fuse would give us
a minute before the dynamite blew. That always seemed like a long time
considering we had to fly in circles and wait for the blast before going in
for another attack. Well clear, we counted the seconds and waited. Then
there was a brilliant flash!

A twenty-ton chunk of compressed snow rose up momentarily then plummeted down the steep slope taking tons of snow with it. The tunnel opening became buried in thirty feet of snow. Already men in huge front loaders and snowploughs were moving towards the opening from their safe location a half mile down the road. It would take the crew all day and well into the night to clear up the mess.

"That bugger isn't going to kill someone in the middle of the night," Marty shouted with glee. "Let's hit the one above the camp."

An hour later, with our mission complete we flew back to Stewart via a longer, safer route.

I was sitting down to supper when the phone rang. It was Marty.

"There's a bloody big cornice ready to break off right above Summit Lake. The rest of my crew were supposed to blow it down with the rocket launcher today. Too far away, the nimrods told me. Now I gotta deal with it," Marty said, sounding more than a little annoyed. "We shouda hit that bugger today,"

"The weather's supposed to hold," I replied. "We can hit it tomorrow."

"Trouble is I've got an all-day meeting with the brass so I'll have to send Phil with you. You OK with that?"

He knew I wasn't OK with that, but I lied and said, "Fine."

Phil was an over-educated enigma who was far more interested in climbing mountains than blasting snow off them. He had long hair, a full beard, dressed sloppily and was far too casual about the serious business of controlling avalanches.

But he was the only person other than Marty who'd dropped bombs from my precious helicopter. I'd once overheard him asking Marty why people treated him like an outcast.

"If you dress like a hippie and act like a hippie, people are going to treat you like a hippie," was Marty's straightforward answer.

The next morning was not only clear, but the wind had died down. Phil arrived late as usual with no apologies forthcoming.

"Great day for flying," I said, trying to be civil.

"Yep," he replied, with a smirk on his face. The smirk turned to annoyance as I doddled a bit getting the helicopter ready for takeoff. His packsack was weighted down with sticks of dynamite, blasting caps and fuse, which he plunked casually on the seat between us like he was getting on a bus to Disneyland.

We took off and followed the route taken yesterday to Summit Lake. A huge cornice, wind-carved and shaped like an unfinished face on Mt. Rushmore, stood a thousand feet above a long, wide avalanche chute directly above the road.

As always Phil's casual demeanour turned to nervousness as soon as we were airborne and his hands shook as he put together a very large bundle of dynamite.

On this almost windless day, it was easy to fly in and hover just a few feet above the cornice, making it a simple target. Phil lit the fuse and tossed the sticks like they were red-hot coals in his hands. He had forgotten to open the sliding plexiglas window on the door. The weight of the dynamite knocked the window out and a gush of cold air hit me.

"He broke the damned window but at least the dynamite is gone," I thought with some sense of relief.

As I peeled away from the cornice, I glanced over at Phil. He had a look of horror on his face.

"The dynamite's landed on the cargo rack," he said, barely above the noise of the engine.

"Phil," I shouted above the roar, "get your bloody ass out there and throw it off!"

He just looked at me through that thick beard and absent-mindedly brushed his hair out of his eyes.

"My god!" I said to myself. "The idiot must have a death wish. He's not doing anything."

All I wanted to do was get away from this crazy bastard. My gut knotted up with fear and I momentarily panicked. Crazy thoughts raced through my brain. "I'll jump out of the helicopter. I'll fly back to the cornice, land and run like hell. If I don't make it at least the day won't be wasted." Then anger and adrenalin brought me back to reality. If I jump out of the helicopter the rotor will probably chop me up. If I land on the cornice I may save some truckers lives on the road, but I would most likely be dead.

The seconds were ticking by fast. This moron sitting beside me was my only hope of living through this.

"Phil, get your ass out there, *now*!" I screamed.

He fumbled with his seat belt.

I grabbed the cyclic with my left hand, abandoning the throttle and collective, flipped his seat belt open and pushed him hard with my right hand. The engine RPM red-lined and the helicopter did some very dangerous gyrations before I could get my hands firmly back on the controls, but I managed to shake Phil out of whatever galaxy he was in. He fiddled with the door and finally opened it. The rotor blast flipped it out of his hands, nearly tearing it off its hinges. He looked down... then back at me.

If looks could kill he would have died right there because that's what he saw on my face. The door was flapping madly in the wind and it whacked him hard on the head. Instead of knocking him senseless, it seemed to have the opposite effect. He climbed reluctantly out on the skid. The fierce wind from the rotor blast blew his hat to oblivion and whipped his long hair into his eyes. White knuckles showed where his right hand gripped the cabin; now the door was beating at his backside. He leaned out of my sight. We had to be out of time. The only good feeling I had was that I knew I wasn't going to feel any pain.

But others would feel pain including my wife who was probably changing diapers on our newly-adopted son, Henry, or preparing supper in the kitchen. My son would grow up without me and if I was lucky he might ask one day about who I was.

Phil was back in the cabin when the blast hit us so hard that he was nearly thrown back out the open door. An updraft more powerful than the one yesterday hit us and sent us surging upward. Hot air poured in through the madly-flapping door, covering us with sooty snow and debris. Then, I realized that it was Phil's incompetence that had saved us. He must have cut the fuse wrong. It had lasted longer than a minute.

I flew slowly and carefully in circles, checking to see if the helicopter was in one piece.

Phil had managed to throw the dynamite off the rack and it had gone off after hitting the avalanche path below us. A huge gaping crater had been blown in the snow, sending its contents cascading down the steep slope, but the main snow pack hadn't budged.

"Damn," I said to myself. "We'll have to do it all over again, but not today, and not with this guy."

I headed for Stewart feeling quite exhausted. Phil, who sat quietly beside me, looked worse. The wind from the broken window ruffled his hair and beard and brought tears to his eyes. Not one word was said between us.

I landed in Stewart and shut the helicopter down. We both just sat there and watched the rotor blades slowly wind to a stop. Then, he quietly grabbed his gear and left.

That night at the King Eddy it was my turn to guzzle beer. Marty was pretty stunned when I told him about the day's events, but he was even more upset when I said, "From now on we use at least five minutes of fuse and no Phil."

"Hank," he moaned, "do you know how much wrapping that is and think of the time wasted."

"Five minutes!" was all I said.

Marty was a smart dude. While we were haggling over how long a fuse should be, he suddenly jumped up, walked to the bar, ordered a jug of beer and plunked it down in front of me.

"How about three minutes, but only when I'm with you," he finally said.

"OK," I replied, laughing for the first time in hours.

The next day, Marty and I flew up and blew a chunk as big as a house off that cornice.

It rolled down the steep slope like a dice on a crap table. As it passed yesterday's crater blast in the snow, a huge crack spread across the whole avalanche path. The crack widened and a ten-foot-deep slab of snow a half-mile wide began to slide down the steep slope in slow motion.

This picture was taken at the moment the dynamite exploded.

In moments, it broke into a million pieces and cascaded down the mountainside, tearing out trees with freight-train force. Plumes of snow rose hundreds of feet in the air. Snow and turbulence engulfed us like a white tornado. I pulled in full power and dove like an osprey to get clear.

"I've been waitin' all my life to see one of those," Marty shouted, looking as excited as I'd ever seen him. Once the clouds of snow cleared, we could see that the sheer momentum of the avalanche had carried it far out onto the Salmon Glacier and obliterated the road for half a mile. It would take days to clear it, but no lives would be lost.

As for me, after the events of the last two days, I was thinking about how I missed the chance to become a tow boat captain.

Note: Phil returned to New Zealand and was killed the following summer in a mountain climbing accident.

CHAPTER FOURTEEN

THE GHOST OF OLD GROWLER

Nestled high on a small plateau next to the meandering Stikine River, the Telegraph Creek townsite sported a church, a small trading post and a Hudson Bay Company store all operated by the few white folk living in town. A small hospital run by a single nurse sat up on the hill next to the village. Like so many mining ghost towns, small shacks littered the town and clung precariously on the sides of the canyon.

This was also the traditional home of the Tahltan Native Indian tribe who'd lived there for countless generations. The town had witnessed the discovery by prospectors of gold on the Stikine River in the 1860s and was the final destination for river boats that had brought men in and gold out. In 1866, the construction of an overland telegraph line to the Yukon had given the town its name. Once the gold rush was over, this vast wilderness area known as Stikine country was home to a huge variety of animals, but it was almost uninhabited by men.

We were all camped on a plateau next to the poorest excuse for a runway I had ever seen. Len's group of prospectors camped in tents. Len was a geologist and a prospector who ran the company that I was contracted to for the summer of 1972.

A year had gone by since Bonnie and I had somewhat reluctantly left Stewart. The base that I had worked so hard to establish had been turned over to another VIH pilot, and I commenced flying out of Victoria. We had purchased another turn-of-the-century house in Victoria, a mere block from the Strait of Juan de Fuca. But here in Telegraph Creek, Brad, my engineer, and I had the luxury of living in a log cabin that we rented for $25.00 a month from a local prospector. The roof only leaked when it rained. Bug specimens that could turn any museum into an entomologist's treasure, inhabited the open cracks in the logs. The mice had long ears, and big doe-like eyes that gave them their deserved name: Deer Mice!

A steep canyon that encased a roaring creek, and an almost-as-steep windy gravel road, separated us from the Indian village and descended several hundred feet to the townsite.

"Let's bum lunch at Shezley," Len said around noon after a long morning of flying in and out of creek bottoms in a Bell 47 G3 B1. It was still one of those two-passenger, 70 mph sloggers, but it had a much wider cabin.

We were always welcome for a bite to eat at Shezley, a mining camp about 30 miles west of Telegraph Creek where I was based for the summer. Len had generously lent them the use of the helicopter when he was off doing groundwork. Unlike our humble dwellings, Shezley was a big mining camp with the luxury of trailers. We landed a good distance from the cookhouse so the dust we raised up wouldn't send the cook into a frenzy. I'd met him a few times and he was a grouchy old bugger with a big meat cleaver.

It was a little early for lunch, so Len headed immediately for the office where he would no doubt trade secrets with one of the Shezley geologists. I stayed behind waiting for the rotor to stop so I could tie it down.

A few men hanging around the bunkhouse started waving. I waved back wondering why the heck they were doing this. Now they were waving and pointing at me. So I waved back and pointed too, beginning to wonder about these men. Finally, a big, older man with a snowy white beard came out of the cookhouse, put his hands around his mouth and shouted at me. All I understood was the words, "Behind you…"

I heard an eerie, guttural groaning sound and turned to look.

A very large grizzly was headed towards me with an awkward loping walk that I knew could turn into a lightning fast run in seconds. I felt like a WWII foot soldier facing a German Panzer tank with nothing but a .303-calibre Lee Enfield rifle. The bear's close-set beady eyes stared cold as a dead arctic char, right at me. Its crooked mouth with long, dagger-like teeth was covered in drool. Its mammoth legs that looked like wind bowed timbers sported long, sharp claws. I had chased grizzlies with the helicopter and had seen them lying like sleeping teddy bears shot full of tranquillizers, but always at a safe distance. Never had I been this close and I was terrified.

"When you encounter a bear, don't turn your back or run, or you'll be dead," all the old prospectors had told me. I could handle the idea of dying, but to be torn to bits first was not my preferred exit choice.

I turned and ran like hell towards the cookhouse. Now, there was not a soul in sight anywhere. At any moment, I expected a clawed paw to rip my back to shreds and strong jaws to bite my head off.

Nothing happened and after what seemed like an eternity, I dove through the kitchen door, landing flat on my face. As I struggled out of breath, a hand reached out and helped me up. It was the old man who'd shouted the warning at me.

"Name's Tom Crouch," he said with a smile on his face. "We call that bear, 'Old Growler's Ghost'. Seems he was more interested in the helicopter than in you. Come have a look."

We joined the cook who stood looking out the window with his meat cleaver in hand.

The bear was wandering around the helicopter sniffing and poking. I can't begin to imagine what was going on in his mind. When he got around to the front, he turned and looked at the big bubble all freshly shined and polished this morning. No doubt he saw the reflection of another bear looking back at him and he took a big swipe at it.

Then, with a bored look in our direction, he wandered off. When he was well clear, I headed for the helicopter with Tom in tow. The very expensive, one-piece bubble had a large jagged crack down the middle, making it unsafe to fly at any speed.

"That bear's been in and out of this camp a dozen times in the last month, usually at night. He makes a weird shrieking, choking sound that makes your hair stand on end," Tom said, picking up a tuft of hair the jagged edge had ripped from the bear's paw.

"I heard it," I said shuddering. I was helplessly staring at the damage, trying to figure what the hell I was going to do.

"I gave him his name from a tale I was told when I was prospectin' outa Stewart back in the late twenties. Trappers and prospectors would come back from the Unuk River, especially around Sulphurets Creek near Tom MacKay Lake, talking about a so-called Phantom Growler. They also mentioned that back in 1923, trapper Jess Sethington of Stewart, B.C., had disappeared mysteriously in the Unuk country."

My heart jumped at the mention of beautiful pristine Tom MacKay Lake. I had spent many hours flying in that area and had heard similar stories, but I let him continue with his tale.

"So many men heard these strange moans and groans and sounds of a large animal crashing through the bushes that they were sure now that it was a very large grizzly.

"He became known as Old Growler and few thought he was harmless. These strange growlings and wanderings at night went on until 1935 when two brothers named Jack and Bruce were working a gold showing in Cripple Creek near Sulphurets.

"Bruce was alone with his dog when a grizzly bear came crashing out of the bushes. The dog attacked the bear and was sent flying, hurt but not killed. This gave Bruce time to grab his rifle and shoot. But the old bear kept coming and Bruce kept shooting until the grizzly lay dead at his feet. Bruce and his brother took the head of the possible 'Phantom of the Unuk' – another name given him – into Ketchikan for examination. The bear's jaw was badly smashed with teeth missing. It was noted there were five old bullets lodged in the skull, which could have been in there for years. Two bullets were .30-.30 calibre and three bullets were .38 calibre which was the same calibre of the rifle and pistol that Jess Sethington was carrying when he vanished in 1923.

"Now this here bear sure isn't related to Old Growler, but it's enough to start a man thinking ghostly thoughts. Most grizzlies ain't night travellers, but this one wanders around this camp at night making strange wheezing, rattling sounds. He hasn't eaten anyone yet that I know about, but he bangs on doors scarin' most of the men half to death. Maybe this bear took a bullet or two as well."

Growing quiet in deep thought, Tom finally said, "Waddya say we eat some of that grub sittin' on the table?"

During lunch, I began to realize the situation I was in. I had an unflyable helicopter and Brad, my engineer with the necessary tools to fix this, was miles away.

Then I remembered that my friend Ron Wells was on his way to Telegraph Creek in a Beech 18, a small 6- to 8-passenger aircraft, pretty much identical to the C-45 Expediter that I'd flown in the Air Force. How he ever made it in and out of that runway at Telegraph Creek in one piece I'll never know. I'd had trouble landing the Expeditor on a wide paved runway 5,000 feet long.

"What's up?" Ron said on the somewhat unreliable single sideband radio, once I'd finally established contact.

When I told Ron what had happened, there was no sound for thirty seconds. It wasn't proper to laugh on an aircraft radio, but he couldn't hide the giggle in his voice when he replied.

"If you promise to keep that bear away from me, I'll pick up your engineer in Telegraph and bring him on over."

"If I see the bear again, I'll ask him to stay away," I replied, and added, "Tell Brad to put down his knitting and bring a drill and lots of locking wire, 'cuz it's sewing time."

Brad arrived with a look on his face that reminded me of my old engineer friend, Ernie Grant.

I could just imagine Ernie saying, "What the frick you done now, Sands," sounding a little fiercer than the new Old Growler.

It took us most of the day to make the helicopter flyable. I drilled holes along the cracks and Brad came along behind like a seamstress, sewing the bubble together with stainless steel locking wire.

It was a good session. I talked and Brad listened, just like Ernie used to. He groaned quite often which I assumed was because he kept sticking himself with the locking wire. We made it back to our leaky cabin at dusk.

The next morning, Len and his crew headed off in his four-wheel-drive truck to check up on road accessible outcroppings. Since I had some free time, I decided to fly down and visit Bobby Ball, thinking he might just know something about this bear.

The Diamond-B Ranch was a hunting camp located right on the Stikine River, but on the opposite side. It was just 5 minutes flying time downstream from the town. I landed in a field well clear of the pack horses that were busy stuffing themselves with the lush grass. Soon Bobby Ball would be making winter guiding trips up in the mountains with them. Bobby looked up from the fence he was mending, waved and headed towards me with a welcoming smile.

I'd first met him in March 1970 almost exactly a year after I'd helped Ron Wells build a runway in Shaft Creek. Once again Ron had gotten himself mired in the snow in his Otter high up on a mountain at one of Bobby's hunting camps. We'd worked together for two days digging Ron out of the snowbank and sending him off. We become friends and he'd been very happy about me spending a summer with him in Telegraph

Creek when he had a little bit of leisure time. Bobby had inherited his famous and prosperous big game hunting lodge from his parents. His wife, Nancy, had worked at the lodge for two years and married him in 1957. Now the two carried on the guiding and hunting operations that his parents had started.

Nancy's work included managing the ranch and feeding and school-ing the kids, while Bobby was the hunting guide who guided the horses up the narrow trails, burdened with wealthy European and American trophy hunters and their gear. As always, when I visited, I was dragged into the house and served a hot cup of coffee from the kettle on huge heavy cast iron wood stove. In the background, I could hear the steady thump of the waterhammer pump, an ingenious device that converted the creek water that gurgled close by the house into a decent flow at the taps. Nancy busied herself cutting fresh homemade bread that would soon join the coffee at the large gouged and chipped oak table where we sat. I told Bobby all about my experience with the Ghost of Old Growler and asked him if he knew of the bear.

"Actually, I heard a strange story about a bear a couple of years ago from Bud Jackson, a guide who dropped in here by boat on his way down-stream," Bobby said squinting with a faraway look. "He told me about having the bad luck of taking this nasty little dentist from New York up on a fall hunt. The guy was oblivious to the beauty of this country and its animals. All he wanted to do was shoot a grizzly and get out of here!

"Apparently, he complained about everything especially the fact that a bear didn't jump out in front of him the first day. Bud said he finally spotted a bear a short distance off on an open avalanche slope. He put binoculars on it and identified it as an adult female that would probably have cubs in the spring. No decent hunting guide is ever gonna shoot one of them.

"While Bud was studying her with the binoculars, the dentist started shooting with his semi-automatic rifle. He got four bullets off before Bud could stop him.

"One of the bullets tore a chunk out of the bear's jaw, spattering blood all over her face and on the ground. The bear took off, possibly mortally wounded. They tracked her until dark. Bud said he spent the night in his sleeping bag with his loaded rifle, hoping the bear would return and tear the dentist and his tent to pieces.

"What became of the dentist?" I asked.

Bobby hesitated, took a long swig on his coffee, then continued, "Bud sent that little weasel packing back to New York without so much as a rabbit. Bud assumed the bear was dead, until the next spring when he heard people around Shezley complaining about losing small pets and chickens and hearing strange sounds at night. So you aren't the only one who's had a run in with that old gal. I just hope she doesn't kill someone. If she's got a damaged mouth it's likely that she can probably only eat soft and easy-to-catch food. Small animals and humans just happen to be soft and easy-to-eat. The thing that bothers me is that if someone gets killed, that dentist will never face any responsibility for it. I've also had my fair share of hunters like that."

A couple of weeks later, I dropped Len and a fellow geologist in a small clearing just a short distance from Shezley. They headed off down the slope to do some mineral exploration and break a few rocks. I shut down and dragged out a book to read. A familiar grunt and groan got my head out of the book fast. Not fifty feet away, stood Old Growler's Ghost, standing up on her haunches behind a low growth of scrub trees. We stared at one another. The only solid thing between us was the newly-replaced and polished bubble. Not only was I in a very dangerous situation, but I had two geologists wondering around, out of contact, totally unaware that a treacherous grizzly bear was close by.

I did the only thing I could do. I put my finger on the starter button hoping that if she decided to attack the noise would scare her off, or all else failing, I could whack her with the rotor. The big head popped out of sight only to reappear a few feet to the left. Then suddenly she came charging at me. I pushed the starter and the engine quickly came to life, but the rotor, as always, was slow to wind up. I pushed the cyclic full forward to tip the rotor blades down as far as possible.

The bear kept coming and I kept forcing the rotor up to enough speed to whack her. At the last second, she veered and ran right by me, heading down the mountain. Fear grabbed me and my gut knotted up! This bear could be a man-eater and I had two geologists wandering around down there. The rotor seemed to take forever to come up to flying speed.

I finally applied collective with only one thought. Find the men and try to scare the bear off. The helicopter, glad to be rid of the weight of two men, popped out of the tree-lined opening with ease.

I was over the edge of the cliff in seconds, searching the steep slope expecting to see the bear tearing up the men, but there was no immediate sign of the bear or the two men. I circled looking behind every tree and bush. Then, I finally spotted the two men and couldn't believe my eyes. They were nothing but dots thousands of feet down the mountain standing on the only flat spot for miles waving their arms frantically. I landed

A grizzly bear or a ghost?

beside them and they scrambled into the helicopter like rabbits with a coyote nipping at their tails.

"Get the hell out of here!" Ken shouted.

I wasn't about to argue with the two huffing, puffing, red-faced men. I wasted no time getting airborne as they scrambled for their seat belts. Once settled into comfortable level flight, they finally filled me in.

"That so-called ghost grizzly of yours came down the mountain like a bloody Brahma bull," Ken shouted over the noise of the engine. "We both ran, or should I say *flew*, down the mountain to the spot where you picked us up. We'd heard the helicopter start up and hoped you'd be looking for us."

Jim added, "We didn't dare look back until we reached the flat spot where you picked us up. Don't know what happened to the bear."

It seems the two of them had been just about as airborne as I was. They'd covered 2,000 feet of steep slope in the time it took me to get there in the helicopter. I think what saved their bacon was that they were scared shitless, powered by pure adrenalin and the fact that bears don't run downhill too well. We searched every square inch of that mountain, but the there was no sign of the bear.

"Let's head for home! I need a stiff drink!" Len finally said.

We followed the Stikine River upstream to Telegraph Creek. Moose who browsed everywhere in swamps fed by the river lifted their heads out of the water to stare at us. Creeks that fed into the Stikine River were dotted with small lakes created by hundreds of hard-working beavers.

The lust for minerals and gold had us return to that area many times, but we never saw the Ghost of Old Growler again.

CHAPTER FIFTEEN

BATTLE FATIGUE

The sun hadn't come up yet as I drove past the Forest Industries Flying Tankers sign and turned down the narrow road to the base at Sproat Lake. I had a new hat on my head with the initials FIFT on the front.

It was August 11, 1976. I'd spent the previous summer flying out of Port Alberni for Vancouver Island Helicopters and had gotten to know Bill Waddington, manager of Flying Tankers. He had not only offered me a job, but the exciting privilege of picking up their first Jet Ranger in Fort Worth, Texas. This time it was the new Jet Ranger B. I had made the trip with my son Jeff who was then fourteen and visiting from Calgary.

The road widened into a shopping-mall-sized tarmac that was the winter home for the last two WWII Martin Mars water bombers in existence. Now they floated a half mile offshore in the early morning mist. Scaffolding and long ladders were stacked against the tall fence that tried to hide the complex from expensive waterfront homes. Large steel boxes

The Martin Mars.

bolted together contained decades-old replacement engines bathed in oil. I drove past the surprisingly small hanger, considering the size of this operation, and parked in front of the aircrew quarters. The eaves were laced with muddy barn swallow nests. The birds darted back and forth gobbling the multitude of mosquitoes that attacked us from the nearby swamps. Just a few feet away in the lake, logs supported long rough-hewn docks. Powerboats of all shapes and sizes were tied up there. Later in the day they would travel back and forth to the Mars with oil, gas and burley men heavy with tools.

Ducks and geese as tame as chickens swam everywhere and walked the docks. Their never-ending droppings made the walkways and ramps slippery as a ski slope. The crew of engineers and pilots would all arrive at noon and stand by until 8 PM. The fire hazard was edging toward extreme.

FIFT was a fire fighting organization and 90% of fires started in the afternoon or evening. I would have to stand by until 8 o'clock and possibly fly until dark if a wildfire started up.

The Jet Ranger sat quietly on the tarmac beside the fuel pumps, waiting for me. Gary was busy doing a walk around checking for leaks, popped rivets or anything else that might make the helicopter unsafe to fly. We were the only two people on the base at this early hour. His primary job was flying the big Mars water bombers. His secondary job was relieving me so that I could get a day or two off. Other than basic training, everything Gary knew about helicopter flying he had learned from me.

He was tall, thin and athletic-looking, liked to eat raw onions and was probably most happy on the edge of stream fishing for steelhead. We took off and headed south following the enormous water pipeline that snaked its way from Great Central Lake, a crystal clear glacier-fed lake several miles north east of the base, into Port Alberni. It supplied millions of gallons of water to the ever-thirsty pulp mill and other industrial complexes crowding the waterfront at the head of the Alberni Canal. The last mile of pipeline travelled through a large salt-water estuary. The superstructure of beams that supported the pipeline over the swamp needed replacing. I intended to teach Gary how to hook up beams under the helicopter and sling them.

Early morning fog was turned into dense smog around the pulp mills smokestacks. We landed at an old log sorting area a half-mile from the pipeline. A huge pile of new beams lay waiting for us. A dozen men stood on the rotting waterline support structure, waiting to receive and install the new wood.

I spread out a thirty-foot length of yacht braid and slipped the large steel ring at one end onto the automatic quick release hook attached to the helicopter. At the other end of the line was a hook that could be electrically released with the simple press of a button inside the helicopter.

Yacht braid, which would not stretch, was now widely used in the helicopter industry for slinging operations. It got its name because it was used commonly on sailboats. Short steel chokers were looped around the beams and would be attached to the automatic hook one at a time. Over the years, there had been many cases of the more elastic nylon rope stretching and breaking. This caused a few accidents when the loose end snapped into the helicopter.

The plan was that Gary would hook me up for the first half-dozen trips, then we would reverse roles. I had little doubt that he would be quite capable of slinging the beams, but like a mother hen I would be watching him closely.

After about the tenth trip a nasty crosswind came up from the canal making it difficult for me to sling the beams into place.

"Dammit," I said to myself. "I have to finish this today. I'm booked solid for at least the next week." So I decided that to do the whole job myself, because Gary didn't have the experience to deal with the difficult crosswind.

A 200-foot-high power line ran parallel to the water line. It carried 130,000 volts of electricity and, like the water line, fed the mill and other industrial complexes. The power line and the water line were a mere stone's throw apart. I would have to fly to within a hair's breath of the power line and make a sharp turn into wind. On the next trip, I turned hard, but the wind fooled me. There was a loud sickening bang and then a brilliant flash of blue-white light engulfed me. The helicopter shuddered like a buck-shot duck whose proud flapping wings were doomed to fail.

The rotors were still turning, but the badly unbalanced machine was in its death throes. My head hit the plexiglas window, leaving me drifting in and out of consciousness. Countless images of my past flashed before my eyes.

"I'm going to die six blocks from where I live!" was my last ghastly thought.

Pain brought me back to consciousness and I realized that I had hit the power line.

My head throbbed and my eyesight was blurred, but I knew I had to put the helicopter blades into a flatter pitch before the damaged rotor broke off and tore the whole machine and me to bits. I was being thrown around inside like a rag doll. A surge of adrenalin sent me thrashing toward the collective and I desperately slammed down on the lever with all my strength. It bottomed out.

The helicopter smoothed out just enough that I could get my trembling hands firmly back on the controls, but now I was heading towards the swamp like a spent meteor. I had only seconds before I had to flare the helicopter in a steep nose-up attitude to speed up the rotation of the rotors and stop my forward flight. The extra stress on the damaged rotor could break it away and I would hit the ground in a mangled heap.

I flared and waited for the crash. The helicopter gradually slowed. Smoke was poring into the cabin and a stomach-churning grinding sound above my head told me the transmission was about to let go. Finally, with all forward flight reduced to zero, I gradually pulled up on the collective to increase the pitch on the rotors and slow my descent. If the helicopter was going to come apart, it would be now. Amazingly, it held together, but I hit hard!

Thankfully, thick swamp grass cushioned my landing, but it left me buried belly deep in mud. As the helicopter ground to a stop, I was aware of the smell of hot oil which mingled with wisps of smoke drifting out of the engine compartment. The main rotor finally stopped in front of me, a bent twisted piece of junk metal. All I wanted to do was close my eyes and wait for the headache to subside, but the wisps of smoke now turned black and started to fill the cabin. I jumped ankle-deep into the salty swampland and staggered towards the water line. The pulp mill crew watched me in dumbfounded silence.

Suddenly, there was a loud *BANG!*

I looked back while on the run, tripped over a log and went flat on my face in the mud. The helicopter was still smoking, but it hadn't blown up. I struggled back up and half-walked, half-crawled to the water line structure where I flopped down on a log, wet, bruised and exhausted.

A kind older voice shouted at me from above, "Better get outa that salt water, son. No need to get electrocuted after what you've been through."

I jumped out of that water like it was full of alligators and climbed painfully and slowly up to the group of men. The older man stepped forward and held out his hand. The rest of the crew just stared at me silently.

"My name's Joe," he said taking my hand in his. "Glad you made it, son. I've radioed the pulp mill. They're sending someone to take you back to your base and organizing a barge to pick up that helicopter before the tide comes in and floats it out to sea."

"Thank you," was all I could think to say as I tried to keep tears from running down my cheeks.

The twisted end of a 200-foot, one-inch thick power line dangled in the water close to the helicopter. There was a dazzling flash followed by another explosion. The power line sparked, hissed and coiled like a snake before it became silent. I noticed Gary walking towards us along the pipeline walkway.

I joined him and, since there was nothing more we could do here, we walked away. I was the first to talk and by this time I was misty eyed.

"How the hell could I screw up like this, Gary?" I said as tears fell.

"Battle fatigue," he replied.

When Gary and I arrived back at the base we knew that they had learned about the accident. Engineers and fellow pilots averted their eyes not knowing what to say. I went straight to the manager's office. Bill, my boss, sat red-faced behind his desk.

He was not only the manager he was also one of the Mars pilots. I stood in front of him soaked to the ass, bruised and covered in mud. I fully expected him to say, "What the hell happened?"

Instead he said gently, "You better go home and put some dry clothes on. We'll talk about it tomorrow."

I drove the winding road back to Port Alberni feeling that a century had gone by since I'd driven this road a mere two hours before. As I passed the pulp mill, I saw the helicopter swaying dangerously as a huge crane lifted it onto a barge. I turned away and drove home. My two kids were playing out in the yard. They ran to me and I hugged them both, tears making lines down my muddy face. As I was leading them towards the house, my son looked up at me with a questioning look.

"Daddy, Daddy," he said, "you're all wet. Did you fall in the lake?"

"And you're all muddy too," my sweet-faced little girl added.

I learned later that there was a new employee at the hydro power station. Each time a red warning light flashed on the monitor, he pushed the reset button. Another transformer blew up and another town lost its power. I rationalized that the extensive power outage was more his fault than mine.

Hundreds of workers were laid off for several days.

As I was filling out the report the next day, Bill joked about the accident, no doubt trying to cheer me up. "Everyone's after your balls for cutting off the power. Better go home and hide."

I went home, but there was no hiding. I spent a badly needed holiday with my family.

The helicopter was sent to Vancouver for repairs. Two weeks later, I flew to Vancouver to bring it home. There it sat on the tarmac all bright and polished as if nothing had happened. Like the time I crashed in the Bugaboos, I'd been sitting around stewing and dreading this flight. Then I remembered what Jim Lapinski had said to me in Calgary eleven years ago: "You were like a horse with a broken leg. A lot have to be put down, but some do survive."

I climbed in, started the engine and watched the rotors coming to life once again. I took off and headed back to Sproat Lake. The helicopter was flying smooth a silk, but I was scared stiff. I held it together and by the time I landed back at base I was fine. Everything went back to the way it was.

A year later, I was scheduled to fly out to the West Coast to sling some equipment into a bush camp. The night before, I bit on a piece of bone and broke a tooth. Since the fire hazard was fairly low, Gary was able to make the flight for me so I could get the quite painful tooth fixed.

I was to learn later that while I sat in the dentist chair, Gary was slinging a cargo net full of chainsaws, axes and other gear needed to cut out a helicopter pad. As he was lowering the net into a small opening on the end of 200-foot line, the helicopter suddenly went out of control. It crashed into the trees and burned, with Gary on board. The consensus was that he'd snagged the net on a tree which then pulled him down in a wide arc. I didn't agree.

An inquest was held several months later, in an attempt to determine the cause of the accident. Gary's wife was there with a lawyer. The company I worked for also had a team of lawyers. The Ministry of Transport was also well represented. There was tense atmosphere in the room and everyone stared at me as I began my presentation. I'd been asked to demonstrate what might have happened out there. All I had was cargo net and a long line similar to the one Gary had used.

I presented a very convincing case that Gary had not simply snagged the net on a tree. Something else had occurred.

Immediately after my demonstration, the doctor who did the autopsy was called up.

"Gary had severe arterial sclerosis and was in danger of a heart attack at any moment when he was killed on August 2nd, 1977," the doctor said to a hushed crowd. He went on to describe the autopsy in great detail. You could just see all the lawyers sag in their seats.

The doctor also added that, if Gary had been given a stress ECG test by running on a treadmill, red lights and alarm bells would have gone off immediately and he would have been rushed off to the hospital for a bypass operation. Every commercial pilot under forty was required to take an annual medical with an MOT-approved doctor. Pilots over forty years old, like Gary, were required to have a medical every six months. Included in the exam was a resting electrocardiogram to check heart function. Stress ECGs on a treadmill were avoided because there had been a few instances where pilots given a stress ECG were grounded because they had a slight heart murmur. Then the onus was on the pilot to prove he was fit to fly, an almost impossible thing to do. The powerful Canadian Airline Pilots Association refused to allow any of its pilots to take the stress test as part of their medical; therefore it was dropped as a political hot potato. The findings at Gary's inquest were inconclusive. The exact cause of the accident was undetermined.

CHAPTER SIXTEEN

DOWN, BUT NOT OUT

It was July 1979. Nearly four years had passed since the power line accident and just a month had gone by since I'd once again picked up a new helicopter in Fort Worth. It was called a Bell 206 Long Ranger and held six passengers plus the pilot.

"We're going to base the Long Ranger permanently at the old sawmill in Chemainus so we don't have to deal with this," my boss told me as he stared out the window.

The fog was so dense that the two Martin Mars aircraft moored on Sproat Lake were almost invisible. I was waiting patiently for it to clear so I could begin my long flying day.

"We'll move you and your family over there if you want."

"Wow, Chemainus, the little town that did. City of Murals," I replied. "We're outta here!"

I knew that Bonnie would be more than happy to leave the fog-bound, pulp mill stench behind.

A few weeks later, my rental truck, loaded to the hilt with our belongings, struggled up 'the Hump' that separates Port Alberni from the far sunnier east coast of Vancouver Island. The family cat was in a cardboard box beside me, slowly tearing it to bits. Bonnie, the kids and the dog followed in a '72 badly-rusted Datsun I'd purchased in Stewart years before.

I laughed at the sign we passed that someone with a sense of humour had hung in the trees: *'Last one out of Port Alberni, turn out the light.'*

"Click," I said, and continued up the hill. We were headed for our newly-purchased hobby farm 4 miles south-west of Duncan, which had been my high school home town 25 years earlier.

Glenora was a large agricultural area bursting with dairy cattle, up and coming vineyards and hundreds of little hobby farms. Ours was only two acres in size, but it had a nice panabode house and a small barn. I was at last able to realize my lifelong dream of getting closer to the land, feel the dirt between my hands, and shovel manure, blisters and all. It had been tough slogging at first. All the back-to-the-land books I'd read made it look easy. I was a very happy pilot and hobby farmer until the phone call from my boss almost a year later in June.

"We need to talk, Hank. Nobody wants to fly with you anymore," he said in a strained voice. "I want you to come up here and we'll talk about it."

Everything else he said simply faded away as I recalled my recent memory lapses. I'd been forgetting the names of familiar places I was flying to. Just a week before I'd nearly had a load of water dropped on me by a Martin Mars because I'd forgotten their radio call telling me they were coming in on the fire directly above where I was flying. Shortly before that I'd been hovering over a fire with the monsoon bucket and pulled the

The Farm,
my son, Henry, with Mirabel the family cow, and
my daughter, Kirsty, with a calf we named Ernie.

cargo release button instead of the water release. The expensive 90-gallon bucket had been destroyed.

"You're suffering from situation depression," the psychiatrist told me a few weeks later. The company paid for testing in an expensive, exclusive facility. It cost them a fortune to obtain a diagnosis I didn't understand.

Then the company hired a local counsellor for me. This man was different. No office, no couch. We'd hang out in his rusty old truck, on friends' lawns, at leaf-covered riverbanks, and we talked about my present life, my childhood, my parents.

"Of course you're depressed," he said, after a few sessions. "Your personal life is a mess, the stress of years of flying and the trauma of accidents have finally caught up to you. You've worked your ass off. I don't know how you lasted this long."

Over the next few weeks, I tried hard to understand how I got to this place in my life. As time went on, I slept better, and felt more relaxed and self-confident. Finally, I was able to say, "I'm ready to go back flying."

"They don't want you back, Hank," my counsellor said. "I've been negotiating on your behalf and you have two choices. You can go on long-term disability, or quit and take a six-month severance package. One thing is for sure: if you go on disability, you'll never fly a helicopter again."

At that moment, I realized that I needed to go back flying to prove I could do it. I accepted the severance package, dragged out my résumé, and started to look for another flying job.

In September, I enrolled in a creative writing class at the local college, committed to one day be a professional writer. Bonnie had gotten a job, was making a good income, and the value of our farm had increased dramatically. Until I found another flying position, I was going to be a gentleman farmer, writer and house 'mum'.

All seemed to go well, until a morning, early in the spring of 1981. I awoke to the sound of the bedroom door opening and I saw my wife walk into the dimly-lit hallway. The luminous dials on the clock said 2 AM. In just four hours the alarm would go off and my wife and two kids would be up and fighting for the bathroom while I made breakfast. Home-grown ham, bacon and eggs were available, but the kids would have corn flakes with fresh milk from the family cow. I never knew what my wife would eat before she headed to her job working in the front office of a local hotel. Once I got the kids off to school there would be the usual farm chores.

I dozed off for what seemed like minutes then woke with a start when a fly buzzing around the room hit the window. The bed beside me was still empty. The clock read 4 AM.

My wife was not in the habit of staying up for hours. I struggled half-dazed into my old dressing gown and headed for the door. The fly buzzing around the room hit the window again reminding me where I was. I made my way downstairs.

Bonnie sat on the couch in her nightgown. She had the same grim, far-away look on her face that had been there for days. My gut tightened in anticipation of the forthcoming conversation.

"What's wrong?" I asked.

"I would like you to leave tonight. I want a divorce and custody of the kids," she said.

"That's a big want list," I replied, amazed that I could joke at a time like this. I added, "If I leave, who's going to do the farm chores, and milk the cow in the morning?"

"Then I'm going to leave. I'll come and get the kids on the weekend," was her abrupt answer.

We stared into space in grim silence.

"You've taken an interest in watching hockey lately," I finally said.

"Well, all you do is write poetry and drink," she replied.

I defiantly grabbed the bottle of scotch from the bar, sloshed a few ounces into a glass and gulped it down.

"My dad and I think you drink too much," she said accusingly.

It was growing light outside, which stole what little light was given off from the macramé-shaded lamp my wife had made.

"I'm going upstairs to pack my things."

I heard her moving around, and hoped the kids wouldn't wake up. Finally, she came down the stairs as I poured another scotch. She was dressed and held the best suitcase we owned. She pretended to ignore me as I took another big gulp of the scotch, and felt a little fire creep into the room. Then, I remembered that the kids and I would be riding our bikes to school together in a few hours because it wasn't safe for them to travel the lonely winding road alone. I put the scotch away thinking I needed to do that for the kids.

"You can tell them when they get up, or I'll tell them when I come to get them on the weekend," Bonnie said, heading for the door. It never occurred to me to ask where she was going to stay.

"Let me help," I replied, taking the suitcase from her. I didn't even notice that I had bare feet until I stepped on a sharp wet rock in the misty gloom.

Back inside the darkened room I stared out the window at the barn still covered with a blue tarp since a recent wind had torn off a lot of shingles. There simply wasn't enough money to put on a new roof. Suddenly, the door slammed open and she re-entered leaving a muddy footpath to the side table. She yanked the macramé lamp's cord out of the wall plug, picked up the lamp and stormed out, leaving me in darkness. I heard the car driving away.

Outside I heard the chirping of birds building their nests. New families were on the way.

CHAPTER SEVENTEEN

A NEW BEGINNING

When Bonnie walked out that door and moved into an apartment, she left me jobless with a farm, two kids, and a cat and a dog to care for. I had to sell the farm and all the animals. That made the kids sad. I couldn't take away their pets too! But what was I to do? Absolutely no one wanted to rent a house to a single male parent with two kids, let alone a dog and cat, as well. I felt like an old truck ready for the junkyard.

Then two great things happened that got me out of the junkyard and moving again. Over time, the counsellor who had helped me out of my depressive state became a good friend. He found me an old, but sturdy, house in Duncan that I could afford to buy. Finally, I had a home for the kids and their pets.

I got a call out of the blue a few weeks later from another old friend, Don McGillivary. He offered me a job flying his personal helicopter. I was flying again!

I had only flown for Don for a few months when I got a call from

Stewart Airport in September 1981. The picture on the left shows the VIH hanger I helped to build way back in the early '70s. The picture on the right is the Trans Provincial Airlines Office located just a few steps north of the hanger. Beside it is a Goose aircraft ready to fly me out of Stewart for the last time.

Vancouver Island Helicopters saying, "We'll have a six-week job up in Stewart if you want it."

It took some doing, but I finally talked Bonnie into babysitting our kids in my house.

It was great to fly once again into Stewart in a Goose aircraft. I spent six fun-filled weeks flying the company's brand new Bell Long Ranger, once again wearing my old beat-up Vancouver Island Helicopters hat. Stewart's long winter of heavy rain and fog in the valleys and ice and snow over the glaciers was about to begin. I landed by the old hanger that I helped build many years before and walked to the trailer that housed the rest of the VIH crew. The weather hadn't changed, but the town sure had since Jan and I first saw it from the bow of the *Northland Prince* almost 15 years earlier. It had free satellite TV, year-round bus service from Terrace and paved roads.

On September 23rd, 1981, I took the VIH hat off forever and made the long trip back to Duncan to resume my duties as a single parent.

This was the last time I flew for Vancouver Island Helicopters.
This is a 6-passenger Bell 206L Long Ranger.

I spent a long lean winter keeping kids fed, scrubbing toilets, doing laundry and mopping floors. Finally in June of 1982 things really perked up. I got a call out of the blue from Doug Green, owner of Tri Western Helicopters. I started flying for him on June 15th. He had two Jet Rangers based in Nanaimo and one Bell 47 B1 based in Qualicum. The Bell 47 was contracted to fly crews from the military base in Nanoose Bay on Vancouver Island to Winchelsea Island. This small forlorn island of rocks and scrub brush was the main military control centre for the huge torpedo range that dominated most of the ocean east of Nanoose Bay on Vancouver Island. If it wasn't for the roof bristling with antennae and radar discs, the concrete control centre and surrounding area could be mistaken for Alcatraz Prison.

Each morning I would fly highly-skilled military officers and technicians out to the island, sit all day and return them to Nanoose at the end of the shift. It was an 8 to 5, Monday to Friday dream flying job, albeit a little boring. Occasionally, I would take off and track down a torpedo that had gone astray or chase boats out of the restricted area. I was home every night and had a babysitter during the day.

In July, I met Linda, an attractive woman 10 years younger than me. She was a Home Economics teacher at Cowichan High School in Duncan. Her cooking classroom had been a woodworking shop when I graduated from the same school in 1956.

She was a single parent like me. She had an 11-year-old daughter named Kevena. Over the summer we got very close and began making plans to blend our families together.

In mid-August, the US Navy's top-secret 'Steam Team' arrived at the Canadian Forces Base in Nanoose Bay. They needed a Jet Ranger and a very experienced pilot for a confidential project, and I was their man. I was suddenly working for the United States Navy! Tom, a younger and less experienced helicopter pilot, took my place flying the Bell 47.

My flying job was to pick up an experimental steam-powered torpedo. Normally, all the spent torpedoes were picked up by a scuba crew working out of a modified landing craft, but this torpedo was different. It was considered to be too hot and dangerous for men to handle up close. It was nick named 'The Steam Machine,' an apt name for an experimental torpedo that was powered by steam. The source of heat that created the steam and just about everything else about the torpedo was top secret. 'The Steam Team', as we came to be called, was made up of a crew of engineers and technicians. They had built a huge 15-foot diameter steel ring that encircled steel wire mesh. It looked just like an oversized version of a fisherman's purse or landing net. Three ten-foot cables were attached to the outer ring, equidistant from each other, and were joined to form a tent-like triangle at the top. All I had to do was attach a lanyard to the cables and I had a big oversized fishnet connected to me. We decided that a hundred-foot line would keep me a safe distance from the torpedo if it blew up.

The whole plan was very similar to a fisherman scooping a big salmon out of the water with a net before it gets off the hook. I practiced several times with a dummy torpedo in Nanoose Bay.

At last, we were ready to go. I had a bright red hat on my head with 'Steam Team' embroidered on it. So much for secrecy!

The steam machine was scheduled to be launched on Friday August 24th, 1982, three days after my 48th birthday. I waited on Winchelsea Island for the mission to begin. My Jet Ranger was sitting on the helicopter pad close by. It was an old 206A model painted orange. The registration on the side was F-OKU which meant it was probably an ex-Okanagan Helicopters machine. It had probably come off the assembly line about the same time as the one I picked up for Klondike Helicopters away back in 1967. Bell had come out with a 206B model in 1970 with a much improved, more powerful Allison engine. Fortunately, the new engine had been installed in this helicopter. As shabby as it looked, it could actually outperform the newer model because it was lighter.

Since there was nothing else to do, while I waited I decided to pick some blackberries. They were long past their prime, but there were still lots available. Bees buzzed around me as I picked the juiciest ones from the spiny branches. The airsickness bag I'd gotten from the helicopter was almost full. The berries were a bit mushed up, but Linda would turn them into a great pie. Or maybe two pies. Our newly-blended family included my daughter, Kirsty, who was now 9 and my son, Henry, who was 12 years old and Linda's daughter, Kevena. The five of us could gobble up a pie in no time.

A sudden gust of wind sent a prickly branch into my backside, breaking into my thoughts. My yelp was drowned out as the portable Motorola radio hanging on my belt crackled to life.

"Hank, we've got a hot one for you to pick up," the dispatcher said. "Better get on it fast, the weather people say that a southeaster is moving in. They've just posted a small craft warning."

I'd learned all about those winds the hard way back in the early sixties when I was a cocky young jet pilot flying out of Comox, a military airbase just north of here. I'd been fishing in an 8-foot punt a half-mile offshore when one of these winds turned the calm sea into whitecaps in minutes. I'd barely made it to shore.

"I'm on my way," I quickly replied to the dispatcher and hurried to the helicopter.

The vast open ocean looked relatively calm, but I knew that wouldn't be for long. The battered old Bell Jet Ranger's rotor was already flapping in the rapidly increasing wind.

I gave the chopper a quick look over. The steel purse net sat beside the helicopter, connected to the hundred-foot lanyard. I hooked it to the helicopter, took the door off, strapped my prickled backside in, set the blackberries on the empty seat beside me and hit the starter. I leaned out of the doorless helicopter and watched the 100 feet of line unravel as I climbed slowly upward. Finally, the net was airborne and I took off from Winchelsea Island and headed south-east out to sea. The military had selected this area in the Georgia Strait for torpedo testing because the ocean floor was quite flat and the water shallow.

It took forever to reach the torpedo. The strong headwind and the 15-foot hoop dragging 100-feet below me slowed me down to a turtle's pace. Below me I could see fish boats and the scuba crew boat scurrying for cover in Nanoose Bay, whitecaps giving chase.

"The torpedo is dead ahead a quarter mile," the radar controller said over the radio. This time it was the real thing and the quiet comfort of the bay was far behind me.

Finally, I spotted it a short distance away looking like an oversized aluminium cigar tube bobbing frantically in the waves. As I hovered close, it seemed to be scurrying in all directions. I realized that I was suffering from disorientation, or what pilots call vertigo. With no out-side visibility when flying an airplane, I had instruments to tell me I was upright even when my mind told me I was flying upside down. There were no instruments in this helicopter to tell me whether I was moving sideways, forward, or backwards. My only reference was rough water and a bobbing torpedo. It was hot, but the steam escaping from its body was whisked away by the white caps.

I leaned out, feeling like I was peering over the edge of a 30-storey skyscraper with no fence. A rare fear of heights gripped me like a vise. My fingers could barely reach the controls. I'm 5 foot 6 inches tall and was born with short arms and legs. That was an asset in the cramped quarters of a jet fighter interceptor, but a long lanky pilot would be better suited to today's task. I was sweating profusely, but the cold draft from the Jet Ranger's rotors whisked it away and left my mouth and body dry as cactus. The torpedo had to be picked up quickly. *It may sink at any time*, I'd been told.

"I can't make it. I can't make it this time!" I screamed to myself. I put every nerve and fibre into this near-impossible task and finally managed to drop the huge hoop beside what seemed like a live fish trying to get away. The hoop slowly sank into the frothy water and I dragged it cautiously under the torpedo, feeling like a cowboy on a bucking unbroken horse. At last, it was centred. I pulled the collective to the red line and the torpedo finally popped out of the water. I had caught my fish! Now free of the cooling effect of the ocean, black smoke gushed out through vents in its sturdy body. I wanted to drop it back in the water and just fly away before the smoking beast could blow a hole in me. I remembered all the bears I'd slung out into the bushes and dropped like garbage when they were shot at many of the camps I'd been in. I could get rid of this thing just as easily. No one would argue with me.

But I hung in there. The Steam Team needed this torpedo desperately. The strong tail wind made for a bumpy, but fast ride into Nanoose Bay. I lowered the now-cooler torpedo into the special holding area reserved for it and returned to Winchelsea Island.

There were many times in my years of flying when I was happy to be safely on the ground. This was one of those times. I just sat in my seat, shaking and watching the rotors flap in the wind. I stared around at the tattered and worn upholstery. It reminded me that this helicopter had been flying almost as long as I had, but, unlike me, all the important moving parts had been changed.

Linda had noticed how wired and edgy I would be after a long day

Home with my new blended family.
From left to right: Kirsty, Linda, Henry, Hank and Kevena in 1983.

of flying. She'd kept saying to me over and over again, "You need to quit flying. If you don't, you won't be here to raise the children."

The decision was mine but I took her advice. Today, I would hang up my battered, old flying hat forever. Tomorrow, Linda and I would commence preparations to open a restaurant.

My job was just about finished. With the southeaster blowing full tilt there would be no more torpedoes to pick up. All I had left to do was fly back to Nanaimo, where the Jet Ranger was stationed, leave the helicopter and drive home to my new family.

But, first I needed a few more blackberries for the pie.

The crows were once again gathering around. I'd knocked them topsy-turvy with the rotor blast when I landed.

"Wow!" I said to them. "That last trip was almost too much fun."

The crows just stared. They were more interested in blackberries than conversation, so I went back to picking and threw a few in their direction.

AUTHOR'S NOTES and ACKNOWLEDGEMENTS

It's quite a thrill to see my name prominently displayed on the front cover of this book saying that I am the author. I may own the stories because they happened to me, but writing it down on paper in readable form and finally getting it turned into a book has involved a large number of very good friends, most of them better writers than me. The chapter titled *A Wolf's Moon* was written over 25 years ago when I was taking a creative writing course in Duncan. The professor gave me an A+ and said, "This is a good story if it's really true." I still have the original, which sat in a dusty box undisturbed for 20 years. I presented the story to my friend, Carla Furlong, a published writer, several years ago. She mentored and helped me and started me on the road to many more chapters. I also joined The Victoria Writers Society and enrolled in their Creative Non-Fiction Group. I cannot thank them enough for the help they gave me.

My special thanks to my wife, Linda, who has lived for years with a grumpy writer. I intend to give her a free autographed copy which she will probably never read, simply because she's already read it over and over in a hundred draft forms, all with misplaced commas.

Also special thanks to Peter Miles. For almost a year he patiently turned up at my house week after week to critique my work. There was no mercy from him at all. On one of my beautifully written pages, he wrote, "You've got to do better than that!!" Beside a particularly drippy line, he wrote, "If you were writing for Harlequin Romance, you'd be fired." On yet another page he wrote, "I do not believe for one second it happened like this." He will also get an autographed copy and his wife will at last get a chance to read these stories.

When my friend, Gary Cooney, offered to read the whole manuscript, I said to him, "Look at the big picture, Gary. Don't waste time looking for misplaced commas." His first comment after he read it was, "Hank, you should change the name of the book to *The Helicopter Pilot Who Fell Flat on His Face and Got Up*." I had written, 'Fallen flat on my face,' in four different chapters. I solved the problem by cutting it to three. Thanks for your advice, Gary.

And thank you to my oldest and dearest friend, Len Box. Len was a navigator and I was a pilot in the RCAF in the early sixties. I got out and became a helicopter pilot. Len did something more sensible. He went to school and became a teacher for 30 years, which gave him the expertise to do an amazing final critique on my book.

Len is a meticulous, determined, detail person, like my wife who was also a teacher. He never let even one paragraph go by without removing or adding a comma or correcting a word or sentence. To say nothing of the fact that the paragraphs were rarely right either. It was like I'd started in grade six grammar and worked my way up with him. Len not only helped me with the book, he also lived part of it. Many years ago, when I hit the power line in Port Alberni, he and his wife Arlene came up from Victoria the very next day to cheer me up.

He will get an autographed copy of my book and, knowing Len as I do, he will read it again and he'll make changes and improvements which I will use in my second printing, should I be that fortunate.

When my neighbour, Don Moffatt, dropped over for a quick visit, I proudly showed him a draft of the book cover. He found a couple of errors, which prompted Linda to ask him if he wanted to proofread the whole book. He replied, "I was hoping you'd ask." Don gave a brilliant and detailed polish to the stories.

My final thanks to Bruce Batchelor, his wife Marsha, and their son Dan, at Agio Publishing House in Victoria. They put this book into readable form.

The reason a lot of the photographs in this book are fuzzy is I had a ten-pound Bell and Howell 3-turret, 16 mm movie camera with a hand crank. Each lens had to be manually set. It was probably a smaller model of the camera they used to make Laurel and Hardy movies. It would hold a 100-foot roll of film which lasted 1 minute and 45 seconds. Each roll cost $17 back in the '60s. I was lucky to get any pictures at all considering there was always something getting in the way of my photographic genius, like a charging grizzly, a love-hungry, one-ton bull moose, or an angry buffalo. They belonged there while my camera and I didn't.

Ernie, my mechanic/engineer in most of the stories, might seem a completely fictional character, but he is actually a composite of dozens of colourful, dedicated men who put a careful eye and a wrench to my helicopters.

Note: for more stories by Hank Sands, check out *www.awolfsmoon.com*.